# 汉英语言中的文化思维模式对比研究

Contrastive Studies on Cultural Thought Patterns in Chinese and English

王耀敏 著

吉林大学出版社
·长春·

图书在版编目(CIP)数据

汉英语言中的文化思维模式对比研究 / 王耀敏著.—
长春:吉林大学出版社,2023.3
ISBN 978-7-5768-1540-5

Ⅰ.①汉… Ⅱ.①王… Ⅲ.①英语—文化语言学—对比研究—汉语 Ⅳ.①H31-05②H1-05

中国国家版本馆 CIP 数据核字(2023)第 049211 号

| 书　　名：汉英语言中的文化思维模式对比研究
| HAN-YING YUYAN ZHONG DE WENHUA SIWEI MOSHI DUIBI YANJIU

作　　者：王耀敏
策划编辑：刘子贵
责任编辑：张宏亮
责任校对：安　斌
装帧设计：海之星电脑图文
出版发行：吉林大学出版社
社　　址：长春市人民大街 4059 号
邮政编码：130021
发行电话：0431-89580028/29/21
网　　址：http://www.jlup.com.cn
电子邮箱：jldxcbs@sina.com
印　　刷：天津和萱印刷有限公司
开　　本：787mm×1092mm　1/16
印　　张：11.5
字　　数：200 千字
版　　次：2023 年 3 月　第 1 版
印　　次：2023 年 3 月　第 1 次
书　　号：ISBN 978-7-5768-1540-5
定　　价：68.00 元

版权所有　翻印必究

# 前　言

　　文化、语言和思维之间的关系一直是语言学界颇有争议而又十分感兴趣的问题，尤其是思维和语言的关系。本书从分析三者关系入手，阐述了中西方的文化思维模式及其在汉英语言中的体现，以及对两种语言的影响，希望通过此研究有效促进中国英语教学。

　　本书首先在援引不同时期代表学者对文化、语言和思维关系的看法基础上总结并阐述了自身观点。由于文化、语言和思维有着密切的关系，在某一文化背景下成长起来的人，其思维模式与处于另一不同的文化背景的人有着或多或少的差异。中西方文化背景差异迥然，这必然造成思维模式上的重大差异。其次，本文对中西方思维模式进行了对比。中国人注重综合思维、统一思维、主体意识思维、直觉思维、形象思维和间接思维，而以英国人为代表的西方人重视分析思维、对立思维、客体意识思维、逻辑思维、抽象思维和直接思维。这些差异自然会体现在传递文化思维模式的工具，即语言中。

　　文章的下一部分分别对两种文化思维模式在语言中的具体体现进行了详细的分析与对比。汉语侧重意合而英语侧重形合；汉语的句子结构为主题-评论式，而英语句子结构为主谓式；汉语更强调动态而英语更强调静态；汉语多用有灵（有生命）主语而英语多用无灵（无生命）主语；汉语多用主动形态而英语习惯用被动形态；汉语的语篇结构常呈现出螺旋式发展模式，而英语的语篇结构趋向于直线式发展模式。

　　在具体分析阐述后，本书指出了文化思维模式的差异对中国英语学习者的负面影响并提出一些建议，希望能有助于中国学生的英语学习和英语教学方法的改进与教学质量的提高。

# Preface

    The author makes a contrast between Chinese and English cultural thought patterns and analyzes their reflection in Chinese and English languages with the intention of trying to contribute to the English learning and teaching in China.

    As the theme is related to the relationship between culture, thought and language, which is a conflicting and interesting problem in the linguistic field, the author first discusses the relationship between them with the introduction of the theories and opinions of some representative scholars dealing with this issue. Then based on this discussion the author puts forward her own view that since language, culture and thought are so closely related to each other, people from different cultural backgrounds will develop different preferences in thought patterns. These diverse thought patterns of different cultures will definitely be reflected in the languages as language is culturally transmitted. Then the author makes a detailed contrast between the two kinds of thought patterns and analyzes their reflection in Chinese and English languages.

    The next part of the article makes a detailed analysis and comparison of the concrete embodiment of the two cultural thinking modes in the languages. Chinese focuses on parataxis while English focuses on parataxis; Chinese sentence structure is theme-critical but English sentence structure is subject-predicate; Chinese emphasizes dynamics while English emphasizes static; In

# Preface

Chinese animate subjects are preferred while in English inanimate subjects are frequently used. In Chinese the active form is often used while in English it is accustomed to using the passive form. Chinese texts show a spiral model of development while English texts show a straight-line model of development.

After a specific analysis, this book points out the negative impact of differences in cultural thinking patterns on Chinese English learners and puts forward some suggestions, hoping to contribute to the improvement of Chinese students' English learning and the improvement of English teaching methods and teaching quality.

# Contents

**Chapter One　Introduction** ······················································ (1)

**Chapter Two　Theories of Relation Between Language, Thought and Culture**
··················································································· (4)

 1. Culture, Thought and Language ································ (4)

 2. Standpoints on Language and Thought ······················ (7)

 3. Thought Patterns ················································ (17)

 4. Cultural Thought Patterns ···································· (18)

**Chapter Three　English and Chinese Cultural Thought Patterns(CTP)** ··· (22)

 1. General Depictions of CTP ···································· (22)

 2. Synthesis VS Analysis(Synthetic/Holistic VS Analytic Thought Patterns) ························································ (28)

 3. Unity VS Dichotomy/Dualism (Unitive VS Dichotomous/Dualistic Thinking) ···························································· (32)

 4. Subjective Consciousness VS Objective Consciousness ············ (38)

 5. Intuition VS Logic ················································ (42)

 6. Imagination and Concreteness VS Abstraction ··············· (49)

 7. Indirectness VS Directness in the Process of Expressing Ideas
··················································································· (52)

**Chapter Four　The Reflection of CTP in Chinese and English Languages**
··················································································· (56)

1. Parataxis VS Hypotaxis …… (56)
　　2. Topic-comment Structure VS Subject-predicate Structure ……… (79)
　　3. Dynamic VS Static Preference …… (86)
　　4. Preference in Applying Animate Subjects VS Inanimate Subjects
　　　…… (90)
　　5. Preference of Active Form VS Passive Form …… (94)
　　6. Spiral Preference VS Linear Preference …… (96)
**Chapter Five　Enlightenment in English Learning and Teaching** ……… (101)
　　1. Interference of Chinese CTP with Chinese EFL (English as a Foreign Language) Learners …… (101)
　　2. Interference with English Sentence Writing by Chinese Learners
　　　…… (101)
　　3. Interference with English Discourse Writing by Chinese Learners
　　　…… (119)
　　4. Suggested Ways of Reducing the Interference by Chinese CTP and Chinese Language …… (126)
**Chapter Six　Conclusion** …… (133)
**Appendix** …… (136)
**References** …… (170)

# Chapter One   Introduction

This book focuses on discussing the Chinese and English cultural thought patterns (CTP) in the two languages and their influences upon the two languages with the intention of contributing to English learning and teaching in China. As is known to all, in the process of English learning, the differences between Chinese and English linguistic structures bring some difficulties for Chinese EFL (English as a Foreign Language) learners. Some Chinese EFL learners especially the beginners may produce English sentences with Chinese structural preferences. This phenomenon is called now as "Chinglish", which is noticed mostly in the facet of language interference. Those differences between the two linguistic structures and the Chinese structural influence on English structures developed by Chinese EFL learners have long been remarked and stressed by many educators and scholars on language studying.

However, in the field of English education, the influences of CTP on the languages and especially on the EFL learning have been overlooked, or seldom discussed, or only mentioned occasionally and partially joined with cultural influences, and yet still remain large room for discussion and studying. The learning and teaching of English as a foreign language is mainly limited to the surface level — the level of words, phrases and grammar. The contrast between the two languages is also mainly confined to this stage.

Nevertheless, the contrast between the two is far more than the structural facet. Mr. Liu Miqing (1991), a famous proponent of cultural linguistics, proposes that the differences between English and Chinese languages are composed of three strata.

The first stratum (also the surface stratum): phonology and morphology.

The second stratum (also the middle stratum): grammar or ways of expression.

The third stratum (also the deep stratum): thought.

Therefore, the contrast in thought keeps the deepest facet among the contrasts between the two languages. At present in China the contrastive study of English and Chinese covers all the three strata above but stresses the first two. In fact, the third stratum is more significant because it influences and is simultaneously reflected in the first two.

In Mr. Liu's opinion (1991), although various language groups share the same or similar logic in thinking, there are different thought patterns among them that will stay statically in mind but be inevitably manifested through language, and in turn, formulate specific ways of expression in different languages. Such expressions derived from differences in thought patterns constitute a hard nut for people from different language groups for communication. Now that the principal aim of English learning is to communicate with others, it shouldn't be restricted to the studying and teaching at the phonological, morphological and grammatical level.

Consequently, learning a language is a lot more than learning the structures and meanings of expressions in the language. English and Chinese CTP are responsible for some distinctive features in their respective languages. Interference may occur if Chinese learners subconsciously bring their CTP into the process of English learning. Accordingly, the author of this book makes a

# Chapter One    Introduction

contrast between Chinese and English CTP in their most prominent features. Continuously their reflections in the two languages are compared. Since the issue is in no way separated from culture, thought and language, their relation has to be discussed and clarified first.

# Chapter Two
# Theories of Relation Between Language, Thought and Culture

## 1. Culture, Thought and Language

Since the topic is related to culture, thought and language, the definition and relation between the three should be made clear first.

### 1.1 Definifion of Culture

Culture has been defined in numerous ways. Its typical definition is given by Edward Tylor (1871) in his *Primitive Culture*, in which he defines culture as "... that complex whole which includes belief, art, morals, law, custom, and any other capabilities and habits acquired by man as a member of society." Generally, it seems to refer to all the human phenomena and human products, including language. In this sense "the relation of language to culture is that of part to whole" (Hudson, R.A, 1980: 83). Bates and Plog define culture as a system of shared beliefs, values, customs, behaviors, and artifacts that the members of a society use to cope with their world and with one another, and that are transmitted from generation to generation through learning.

This definition includes not only patterns of behavior but also patterns of thought (shared meanings that the members of a society attach to various phenomena natural and intellectual, including religion and ideologies), artifacts (tools, potteries, houses, machines, works of art), and the culturally transmitted skills and techniques used to make the artifacts (1990:

# Chapter Two    Theories of Relation Between Language, Thought and Culture

28). This definition is close to that of Corder S. Pit's (1967). As a well-known applied linguist, he defines culture in the way that "members of the community share sets of beliefs, political or ethical, they share to a large extent the way they construe the world, how they classify objective phenomena, what meaning they give to this classification". Communities share a common history and agree about what is or is not important to them, that is, a common value system. They agree about the right and wrong ways of getting things done, of dressing, eating, marrying, worshipping, educating their young and so on. All these things are their culture (Corder, 1967:68). Obviously, this view has been influenced by the work of anthropologists who tend to treat language as one element among others, such as beliefs, within the definition of culture as socially acquired knowledge.

## 1.2 Definition of Thought

In the study of the world's cultures, it has become clear that different tribes not only have different languages, they also have different worldviews and thoughts, which are reflected in their languages. In *Encyclopedia* thought or thinking involves mentally manipulating information, as when we form concepts, engage in problem solving, reason and make decisions. Thinking is a higher cognitive function and the analysis of thinking process is part of cognitive psychology. In general, thought is the process of reflecting on the objective world with concepts, judgments, and reasoning. It is considered part of culture.

A Chinese scholar Di Yanhua (2002) argues in her book *American culture* that culture can be seen from two aspects—"subjective culture" and "objective culture". Subjective culture embodies the psychological features of culture, including assumptions, values, and patterns of thinking. Objective culture refers to the institutions and artifacts of a culture, such as its economic system, social customs, political structures and arts, crafts, and literature. Objective culture can be treated as an externalization of subjective culture that usually becomes reified. Therefore, thought can be regarded as the psychological aspect of culture.

There is a close relationship between language and culture. Culture contains language and affects it, which is the environment in which language is formed. Language is an important carrier of culture and an indispensable tool to preserve, communicate and reflect culture. English and Chinese are two highly developed languages, belonging to the Indo-European family and the Sino-Tibetan family respectively. People who use English and Chinese live in different regions. Different regions nurture different nationalities, and different nationalities create different national cultures.

## 1.3 Definition of Language

Language is acquired or learned, by virtue of one's membership of a particular society. It is generally thought that language is the carrier of culture and a vehicle by which the other facets of the culture are communicated. There is no doubt that one's knowledge of his or her native language is culturally transmitted and culture-based. In this sense, it can be said that it is not language that determines culture but that culture determines language. Furthermore, language is influenced and shaped by culture and reflects culture. When grown up, language definitely exerts impact upon culture, for culture depends upon a particular language to realize its functions as recording, cognizing (or cognitive), propagating, cultivation (or educating), coagulating, and regulating.

Language helps people understand not only one another but culture as well, for it is a reflection of culture. If one is to use a language well, one must know the culture in which the language is used. People's perception of the universe shifts from tongue to tongue, and the forms of the shifting are worth considering. Every kind of language will reflect the specific culture of the people who speak the language, and in turn language usage follows culturally determined patterns when language structures, discourse patterns,

# Chapter Two  Theories of Relation Between Language, Thought and Culture

communicative styles and so on all bear a distinct cultural imprint.

In this sense, learning a foreign language means more than merely mastering the pronunciation, grammar, words and idioms as listed in dictionaries and grammar books. It means learning to see the world as native speakers of that language see it, learning the culture — specific ways in which their language reflects the ideas, customs, and behavior of their society, and learning to understand their "language of the mind" (Deng Yanchang, 1989: 4). Therefore, language is not only the carrier of culture, but also inevitably the carrier of thought.

From this point of view, culture, thought and language are interrelated and have become the focus of the study. Saussure, Boas, Sapir, Whorf and some other scholars have exerted an active and animating influence on both speculation and research. Generally speaking, the current understanding is that language, thought and culture are interrelated, and can not operate independently. It has been widely accepted that language, thought and culture are closely related and intimately bound together. While on the relationship between language and thought, different linguists and scholars possess diverse opinions. Here are some of the arguments focusing on the relationship between the two.

## 2. Standpoints on Language and Thought

The problem concerning the relationship between language and thought has been a major issue of philosophy for more than two thousand years. It has occupied philosophers, linguists, anthropologists and psychologists and has been a challenge to them for centuries. The extent to which language and thought influence each other and which is the dominant aspect of communication, has been a matter of controversy for a very long time. In modern times they are discussed within different yet interrelated disciplines. The problem of language and thought can be discussed in two dimensions, i.

e., linguistically or philosophically. Here the two issues will be discussed together and inter-disciplinarily by introducing the various standpoints of some most well-known philosophers and linguists on this issue.

### 2.1 Plato Standpoint

The discussion about language and thought in the West has a long history, which can be traced back to ancient Greece. Greek philosopher Plato proposes that "thinking is talking to oneself, or is a form of monologue. Without thinking, language would be meaningless; without language, thought would have no form and would not be known to others" (Hu Zhuanglin, Liu Runqing, Li Yanfu, 1987:237). Language can be regarded as the dress of thought and thought is wordless language. Therefore, language and thought are inseparable. Thought is language in a sense. This monistic view is further expounded by Saussure.

### 2.2 Saussure's Standpoint

Saussure is famous for his doctrine of signal (signifier or significant) and signification (signified) (1960). The two together form a sign, the basic linguistic unit. He conceives language as a system of signs. Each sign, in turn, has two inseparable components like the two sides of the same coin: an image-carrying form, which he calls the signifier, and a concept or idea signified by that form, which he terms the signified. Saussure roundly denies the possibility of prelinguistic thought. He claims that "we need to learn a language before we can entertain fully developed thoughts. So, our language determines the way of how our ideas about the world are structured, whether or not we express these ideas to other people". For Saussure, the study of language is the study of one aspect of the human mind: a series of mental sound images, and the concepts we have learnt to associate with them (Meng Jiangang, 2003). In a way, thought is dependent on language.

# Chapter Two  Theories of Relation Between Language, Thought and Culture

### 2.3  Wittgenstein's Standpoint

Austrian philosopher Ludwig Wittgenstein is more careful than Saussure about the possibility of thought without language. He appears to hold that certain simple forms of thought are possible even for creatures without language. But other forms that require a structural complexity must depend upon language, because only language can afford something corresponding to the thought. The example he presents is both interesting and significant: "A dog believes his master is at the door. But can he also believe his master will come the day after tomorrow?" (Wittgenstein, 1958) In plain words it can be said that when a dog "believes" something temporally and spatially, it may "think" without language, but it can not "think about" something remote. Thinking is not, for Wittgenstein, some kind of inner monologue.

### 2.4  Aristotle's Standpoint

Another well-known Greek philosopher Aristotle holds a completely opposite opinion, pronouncing that "Words spoken are symbols or signs of affections or impressions of the soul; written words are the signs of words spoken. As writing, so also is speech not the same for all races of men. But the mental affections themselves, of which these words are primarily signs, are the same for the whole of mankind, as are also the objects of which those affections are representations or likenesses, images, copies." (Zeno Vendler, 1977) According to the Aristotelian view, words come logically and psychologically last in a natural order of progression, which begins with the "objects" of the real world. If there were no such objects, human beings would have no "representations" of them in the form of "mental affections"; and if there were no such mental affections there would in turn be nothing for words to be signs of. Aristotle allows a link between thought and language. Any vocal noise which is not the sign of a mental affection is simply not a word, and hence not part of language. Correspondingly, it will always make sense, in

Aristotelian terms, to ask what thought a word expresses, and to identify the thought in question becomes a standard way of explaining what the word means. For Aristotle, language is only the symbol or sign of thought and thought in no way equals language.

### 2.5 Wilhelm von Humboldt's and Franz Boas's Standpoints

Humboldt, a famous German linguist, philosopher and founder of general linguistics, asserts that "The spiritual traits and the structure of the language of a people are so intimately blended that, given either of the two, one should be able to derive the other from it to the fullest extent… Language is the outward manifestation of the spirit of people; their language is their spirit, and their spirit is their language; it is difficult to imagine any two things more identical." (Salzmann, 1998:39) The extent of closeness between language and thought stated by Humboldt is perhaps over-exaggerated, but he points out the notion that the two are indissociable. He also notices that language and thought influence each other. In addition, he gives great importance to the diversity of the world's languages and cultures. He studies language under specific cultural background and thinks that no nation can avoid injecting their subjective consciousness into their language to form a special "world view" in the language, which would in turn restrict people's language usage. Thus, language is considered as a kind of worldview in his theory. He puts forward the idea that different people speak differently because they think differently, and that they think differently because their language offers them different ways of expressing the world around them.

Franz Boas is one of the pioneers of American anthropology. Although he does not directly touch upon the language-thought relationship, he explains the cultural influence (which naturally includes the influence of the thought) on language in this way: "it does not seem likely, therefore, that there is any direct relation between the culture of a tribe and the language they speak,

# Chapter Two  Theories of Relation Between Language, Thought and Culture

except in so far as the form of the language will be molded by the state of the culture, but not in so far as a certain state of culture is conditioned by morphological traits of the language." (Franz Boas, 1911:38) He feels that culture exerts more influence on language, instead of vice versa. In short, on the relationship between language and thought, Boas advocates that a language reflects a culture and that differences between languages stem from differences in cultural backgrounds.

## 2.6  Chomsky's Standpoint

It seems that Chomsky is concerned with how language and thought interact rather than whether they interact or whether one determines the other. In terms of language, Chomsky infers that there must exist some inner or innate faculty for language. Such account of language acquisition has become known as the "Innateness Hypothesis" (Meng Jiangang, 2003). On the issue of language and thought, he thinks the question has already got an answer to it. He wonders why the conclusion should be resurrected centuries later as an audacious and innovative proposal. For him, "thought and language are properties of organized matter — in this case, mostly the brain, not the kidney or the foot." (Chomsky, 1966) The "organized matter" is the brain, and "thought in humans 'is a property of the nervous system, or rather of the brain'."(Chomsky, 2000) According to this theory, the inner language is not learned, but emerges as a part of the genetic heritage, and it is prior to any spoken language. It seems that the innate language faculty determines thought.

## 2.7  Edward Sapir's and Benjamin Lee Whorf's Standpoints

On discussing the relation between language and thought, the Sapir-Whorf hypothesis must be the most famous theory in this field. This theory can be dated back to the notion of Wilhelm von Humboldt and Franz Boas who held similar opinions. But this hypothesis tends to go to the extremes. Since its inception in the 1920s and 1930s, it has caused controversy and spawned research in a variety of disciplines including linguistics, psychology, philosophy, anthropology, and education. It was rooted in American anthropologist and linguist Sapir's study of Native American Languages, which later drew the particular attention of Sapir's student Benjamin Lee Whorf. Having studied Hopi, a major Amerindian language, and touched upon Sanskrit and Japanese, Whorf formed his views on the relation between language, thought, and culture, which were later labeled as the "Sapir-Whorf Hypothesis". Stuart Chase (1955) asserts that it includes two cardinal hypotheses.

First, that all higher levels of thinking are dependent on language.

Second, that the structure of the language one habitually uses influences the manner in which one understands his environment.

Indeed, this summary grasps the gist of the Whorf's views on linguistics and the world. In general, the Sapir-Whorf hypotheses make the claim that the structure of the language one habitually uses influences the manner in which one thinks and behaves. It perceives language as a pair of glasses with more or less warped lenses through which the surroundings are viewed. This hypothesis is described as consisting of two assumptions: linguistic determinism and linguistic relativity.

i. Linguistic Determinism

This notion posits that the way the language is organized will determine how people perceive the world being organized. That is, the language will give people a ready-made system of categorizing what they perceive, and as a consequence, they will be led to perceive the world around them only in those categories.

Edward Sapir maintains that the "relation between language and experience is often misunderstood. Language is not merely a more or less

## Chapter Two  Theories of Relation Between Language, Thought and Culture

systematic inventory of the various items of experience which seem relevant to the individual, as is so often naively assumed, but is also a self-contained, creative symbolic organization, which not only refers to experience largely acquired without its help but actually defines experience for us by reason of its formal completeness and because of our unconscious projection of its implicit expectations into the field of experience." (Sapir, 1931:578) Sapir adds that the force of this claim could be realized only when the relatively similar Indo-European languages are compared with widely differing languages such as those indigenous to Africa and America.

Benjamin Lee Whorf in a series of papers has developed Sapir's claim, maintaining that a language constitutes a sort of logic, a general frame of reference, and so molds the thought of its habitual users. It can be revealed from Whorf's own words: "It was found that the background linguistic system (in other words, the grammar) of each language is not merely reproducing instrument for voicing ideas, but rather is itself the shaper of ideas, the program and guide for the individual's mental activity, for his analysis of impressions, for his synthesis of his mental stock in trade....." (Carroll, 1956: 212)

This theory in its strongest version holds that language determines thought or certain nonlinguistic cognitive processes. In short, one can only think in the categories that one's language allows him/her to think in. In other words, the language people speak determines the way they interpret the world around them (or the way one thinks is determined by the language one speaks). That is, learning a language changes the way a person thinks. Just as Fritz Mauthner in 1902 declared that "if Aristotle had spoken Chinese or Dakota, his logic and his categories would have been different." (Coseriu, 1958:7)

ii. Linguistic Relativity

Whorf himself explains "linguistic relativity" as follows.

...the "linguistic relativity principle," which means, in informal terms, that users of markedly different grammar are pointed by their grammar toward different types of observations and different evaluations of externally similar acts of observations, and hence are not equivalent as observers but must arrive at somewhat different views of the world.(Carroll, 1956:221)

This statement can be interpreted as the cognitive processes that are determined are different for different languages and there are cultural differences in the semantic associations evoked by seemingly common concepts. Thus, speakers of different languages are said to think in different ways and differences among languages must be reflected in the differences of the worldviews of their speakers. Since every language has a form and no two forms are the same, it follows that no two cultures having different languages can have identical views of the world. His views of linguistic relativity should include two essentials.

First, every language is different from others; each language displays the continuum in a different way, but no language is primitive. It is a common sense to point out that every language is different. However, it is noteworthy to assert that no language is primitive. That is the cultural significance of Whorf's hypothesis, which is generally ignored by linguistic analysis.

The second essential is his ideal of "human brotherhood" (Carroll, 1956), which stems from his Christian belief. Although he is aware of the difficulty in communication between different languages and cultures, he hopes "brotherhood" would be achieved, through understanding of language. Obviously, this view is deeply rooted in Christianity.

The opinions of all the previous scholars have been questioned to a certain extent. Yet, they may not be totally negated. It is now universally acknowledged that there does exist a certain kind of relation and interplay between language and thought, although to what extent the structure of one's language shapes one's view of the world thus remains an unresolved issue. Despite all these arguments, there is a growing consensus that language and thought influence each other. Language changes along with the evolution of thought and vice versa.

Professor Gui Shichun from Guangzhou Foreign Language College concludes in his *Psycholinguistics* that language and thought are so closely related that the relation between them is rather complicated, both of which could not exist independently without society. Language and thought are generated and developed through contacting and interacting with the human beings and the social environment. They possess their own rules and principles respectively as well as the rules of interaction (Gui Shichun, 1985).

In the opinion of the author of this book, it would be as absurd or useless as arguing whether chicks or eggs have come into being first to say whether language determines thought or vice versa in extreme terms. Although it is generally acknowledged that language and thought do not come into being at the same time, it is of no significance to discuss which one comes first. In fact, they have developed together and interacted with each other. While in their interaction, thought takes the leading position. Language usage follows culturally determined patterns, which not only influence the order in which people use words to form phrases, but also influence thinking. The English author George Orwell advances much the same proposition that "if thought corrupts language, language can also corrupt thought." (George Orwell, 1946)

## 2.8 Summary in Different Standpoints

In conclusion, language and thought are inextricably linked with each other. Foreign scholars have studied the relationship between the two for a long time, and put forward some conclusions about the relationship between them. The most influential views can be concluded as follows.

1. It is the theory that language determines thinking/thought. That is to

say, different languages determine different cognitive styles, on the basis of which different world views and ways of thinking are formed. This view has received some support, but it has also been widely questioned.

2. Language is the same as thought. That is to say, thinking, like language, is also a habit. Thinking is a silent language, and language is vocal thinking. This view is influential, but it is also controversial.

3. Thinking/Thought determines language. Through the analysis of the stage of children's thinking development, this view holds that thinking/thought precedes language and determines the development of language. This view does not completely solve the problem of the relationship between language and thought.

4. Language and thought are independent of each other and interact with each other. That is, it emphasizes that thinking determines language, but it also admits that the development of thinking/thought is restricted by language. At the same time, it is considered that the two should not be equated, and verbal thinking can not include all forms of thinking. This view has been widely accepted by the international academic circles at present, but it also makes the academic circles involved in a more heated debate.

It can be seen that there are many disputes about the relationship between language and thought. From the above point of view, language and thought are closely related. Once language is isolated from thinking/thought, it becomes a messy and empty note of meaninglessness and with no logic, and is no longer a tool to convey ideas. Thinking/Thought without language, will lose the most vitality, the most intuitive, and the most detailed carrier of the expression of ideas. It can be said that thinking/thought plays a leading role in the two relationships, and it can also be said that thinking/thought determines language to a certain extent, and language affects thinking/thought to a great extent. Thinking/thought and language not just depend on each other, but also interact and influence each other.

# Chapter Two   Theories of Relation Between Language, Thought and Culture

Thinking/Thought is the indirect and general reflection of the human brain to objective things, and it is a process in which people adopt a certain mode of thinking/thought to analyze, sort out, identify, digest, and synthesize items and so on. On the one hand, thinking/thought is closely related to language. Without thinking/thought, language will not have versatility and richness. On the one hand, thinking/thought can not determine its shape and form, and can not prove the truth if there is without the help of language. In this sense, it can be said that there is no thinking/thought without language. Besides, thinking/thought also plays a role in controlling language to some extent. The selection and organization of language materials, the observance of language norms and the organization of discourse structure are all controlled by thinking/thought.

Among the many factors that affect second language acquisition and language communication, the form of language thinking/thought is an important one. Whether to use mother tongue thinking/thought or foreign language thinking/thought directly affects the effect of language learning and the quality of language output. The difference in thinking/thought patterns is an important factor in the formation of distinctive languages.

## 3.Thought Patterns

Thought Patterns refer to the habit or the program of thinking. Different thought patterns are closely interrelated. People employ various thought patterns when solving problems. They may prefer one to another because of the requirements of their vocations or characters. As language and thought are closely related to and influence each other, it is valid to remark that at least part of the reason why people have different linguistic forms and compositions is due to their differences in patterns of thought.

It is natural for people to assume that thought patterns of people in a nation will determine certain choices of their language patterns or communicative styles while some characteristics of the language of people in a nation are a reflection of their thought patterns. Patterns in the mind map a person's life experiences, and in turn experiences verify patterns of the mind. Language acquisition process, one of human beings' most valuable experiences, reflects the distinction in thought.

In a narrow sense, each individual has his own personal preference in patterns of thought, which experiencing the processes learned from birth and contributing to the development of his habitual linguistic style distinctive from others. In a broad sense, thought patterns are culturally determined and they are the deep essence of human cultures. Any racial group has the ability to develop the advanced level of thinking, but in different cultural traditions people differ in those patterns of thought. They vary from culture to culture, sometimes dramatically.

## 4. Cultural Thought patlerns

People within a common cultural background develop some common thought patterns. These thought patterns, which are formulated in the mental process of receiving, reflecting, considering and processing outside information by a certain group of people within a particular society, are called cultural thought patterns (CTP). Once coming into being, these CTP become spiritual characteristics shared by people inside the society and will pass from generation to generation as the most stable or the core factor of the people's cultural traditions. They contribute to the construction of the particular linguistic patterns different from those used by people from other cultural backgrounds with different CTP. It is supposed that all normal human babies are capable of any of the thought patterns ever used in the whole history of human existence, but babies learn to think in patterns that their world shows them. If they are fortunate enough to have more than one culture in their socializing process, they will learn more patterns than their monocultural

# Chapter Two   Theories of Relation Between Language, Thought and Culture

counterparts. It is remarkable to watch someone moving from one culture into another and to discern the difference in an individual's pattern of thought that the cultural change brings. This book just focuses on this broad sense.

Since thought patterns vary from culture to culture, as is known to all, sometimes dramatically, some scholars try to find how they influence the languages in different cultural backgrounds. Among the scholars who have examined and certified this circumstance, Robert B. Kaplan is a representative. He reveals in his paper "Cultural Thought Pattern in Intercultural Education" that "each language and each culture has a paragraph order unique to itself, and that part of the learning of a particular language is the mastering of its logical system" (Kaplan, 1966). Here "logical system" refers to the cultural thought patterns associated with one language. He studied the writings in English written by students coming from five different language groups including English. It turned out that students from different language groups tend to produce passages with five different kinds of paragraph orders.

Kaplan's research firmly asserts that with different CTP people tend to produce different linguistic patterns. Although in modern times, traditional cultural thought patterns are often undergoing changes due to influence of foreign cultures, it is true that they remain the most innate or deeply rooted component of a culture.

The way of thinking reflects the language psychological tendency formed by the ethnic groups of a certain language for thousands of years. There is a great difference in the way of thinking between English and Chinese, which is closely related to the physical and geographical conditions, as well as social and cultural backgrounds of the English and Chinese people. Due to the different natural and geographical environment, English and Chinese people have formed their own national cultural atmosphere and distinctive cultural way of thinking. China is located in the Asian continent and develops in a closed geographical environment. Due to less pressure from nature, people pay attention to the right time, geographical location and harmony. They gradually form the philosophical view of the unity of man and nature, which tends to regard the world as an indivisible organic whole and is used to understanding things as a whole.

The Anglo-American nation is located in a maritime climate, often accompanied by tsunamis, strong winds, torrential rains, earthquakes and other turbulent adverse environment and bad climate. This gradually forms their strong desire to conquer and control by paying attention to space expansion and conquering others by force. At the same time, the unique cosmology and world outlook of Westerners have been gradually formed, that is, the universe is divided into two completely different worlds. Everything in the world is opposed to each other, and the opposition between heaven and earth, man and nature, matter and spirit is emphasized. It is a cosmological view of the separation of heaven and man.

Different ways of life not only form different world views and cosmology, but also form different material cultures. They also give rise to different values, beliefs and interests. From the perspective of cultural origin, Chinese culture has a long history and has been inherited for thousands of years. Buddhism is the only foreign factor in traditional cultures. There are three main sources of Western cultures: Greek culture, Jewish culture and modern industrialism. Western cultures are formed by the confluence of many kinds of national cultures. The economic basis of the emergence and development of Chinese traditional culture is agricultural economy, which has strong closeness and introversion, and which pursues the unity of man and nature and conforms to nature. This makes Chinese traditional cultures embark on the road of introspection and internal pursuit from the date of its birth.

The emergence and development of Western cultures is based on the commodity economy, which is characterized by the exchange of needed goods, openness and extroversion. The European culture produced on this economic

# Chapter Two  Theories of Relation Between Language, Thought and Culture

basis also has the characteristics of extroversion and openness. The way of thinking produced under different cultural backgrounds will naturally be influenced by their own cultural traditions, showing completely different characteristics of thinking.

Language and thinking are inseparable. Language is the carrier of thinking and the abstraction of reality, while thinking is the conscious activity of the human brain to reflect and recognize objective facts. The law of language is grammar, and the law of thinking is logic. Language and thinking influence, interact and represent each other. Language is the externalization of thinking. As Sapir said that language, as a structure, its inner side is the form of thinking. The main results are as follows: when language expresses thinking, it reveals the characteristics of thinking to a great extent, and thus expresses the structure of the human mind. However, without thinking, language will become an empty voice and is no longer a communication tool with the combination of sound and meaning. In fact, the world revealed by language is a world processed by thinking activities. Without the addition of thinking activities, language is only some primitive, disorganized and illogical material. Similarly, thinking is inseparable from language, without language, thinking can not be fixed.

There are distinguishing features in English and Chinese languages, which are closely related to the different cultural thinking patterns of English and Chinese nations. The distinction in thinking patterns has certain influence on the two languages. This book begins with the origin of the generation of the differences in English and Chinese thinking patterns of the two nations. It places emphasis on the major differences in English and Chinese thinking patterns and their reflection on the two languages.

# Chapter Three
# Chinese and English Cultural Thought Patterns

## 1. General Depictions of CTP

In order to find out how cultural thought patterns affect the use of language, the author of this book will try to elucidate the Chinese and English Cultural Thought Patterns (CTP) in this chapter. Before discussing the details of the two sets of CTP in China and the West, it is imperative to point out two facets.

For one thing, any attempt to present CTP inevitably sacrifices specific details and the unique variations within each individual or certain group. No two individuals or groups hold identical beliefs and manifest uniform behaviors, and whatever characterizations reviewed in one culture or cultural group must be thought of as normative tendencies that vary rather than monolithic and uniform attributes. For another, one thought pattern might exist in various groups. That is, it is likely to be found in two totally different cultures.

Consequently, CTP in different nations should be viewed as differing in degree or in emphasis rather than as strictly dichotomous in substance. Therefore, one nation preferring certain kinds of CTP doesn't necessarily mean it doesn't cover others. In other words, though these thought patterns are labeled as Westerners (English) or Chinese, it is not at all the case that

## Chapter Three  Chinese and English Cultural Thought Patterns

Chinese can only think in one set of thought patterns and the Westerners another set. In fact, all the thought patterns can be found in both the two. The distinction is whether those thought patterns have developed to a higher degree or put emphasis on, namely, their difference of orientation in thought patterns is not one in essence, but merely one of degree or extent. After identifying those two aspects, some details will be mentioned about the different preferences in thought patterns between China and the West.

On account of what has been discussed previously, Cultural Thought Patterns in one cultural background are more or less different from those in another. This book only focuses on those that characterize one nation and differ greatly from one another and on those that are closely related to languages. Since the issue of thought is initially and basically studied in philosophical field, the author of this book will discuss the CTP philosophically as well as culturally.

As a group, the Westerners mainly follow the Greek and Judeo-Christian philosophical and religious traditions. Ancient Greece has influenced western thinking ever since the $5^{th}$ century B.C. The ancient Greek notion of mind that we now call deep structure and the affirmation of its individual locus of judgment and decision-making are firmly in place in western culture. It is the stability of the physical world yielded by thought-driven patterns of perception and thinking that stands out in western cultural thought.

Chinese culture has been influenced mainly by such religious and philosophical systems as Confucianism, Taoism and Buddhism, which profoundly affect Chinese people's thinking. Definitely these traditions and religions in China and the West will have a deep effect on the two sets of thought patterns.

From the aspect of cultures, the three pillars of Western culture are science, law and religion. It can be seen that its culture attaches importance to science, through abstract symbols, the use of analytical and empirical methods to make a rational understanding of things, the purpose of which is to seek the truth. There are two cornerstones of Chinese culture: morality and art. Its culture attaches importance to art, through specific and vivid images and the finishing touch to express their feelings and value judgment, the purpose of which is the appreciation and creation of value.

From a philosophical point of view, the traditional Western philosophy talks about "the dichotomy of God" and "the dichotomy of subject and object", which advocates the "separation of characters", and the opposition between matter and spirit, society and nature, essence and phenomenon. At the same time, it emphasizes scientific experiments, paying attention to formal argumentation, advocating individual thinking, and holding that the whole can exist only in individual opposition. It pays more attention to the external expression of logic and praises logic and rationality.

Different from the rational tradition in Western traditional philosophy, the three philosophies that have the greatest influence on the Chinese way of thinking——Confucianism, Taoism and Chinese Buddhism all attach importance to understanding. They advocate "the unity of man and nature", "the blending of things","harmony", and "enlightenment".

These philosophical thoughts have a great influence on the Chinese people's way of thinking which emphasizes "implication" and even "implication". At the same time, seek perfection, perfection, harmony, symmetry and balance, personal feelings and understanding, psychological time and space and time sequence.

It can be seen that the Western mode of thinking is characterized by logic, analysis and linearity. The Western nation has the distinct characteristics of rationality, re-analysis and complete form in the form of thinking. Reflected in language, it is paratactic. For instance, impersonal subjects are often used. Passive sentences are frequently utilized. Subjects are generally not omitted. Conjunctions and prepositions are often used.

# Chapter Three  Chinese and English Cultural Thought Patterns

Generally speaking, the Chinese mode of thinking emphasizes the whole, the understanding and the subject consciousness. This mode of thinking, reflected in the Chinese language, is that Chinese has gradually formed a linguistic structural feature of paying attention to internal relations, implied relations and fuzzy relations in sentence making and textual writing.

It is prominently manifested in the construction of Chinese sentences, which are connected with few or no formal words, but based on the sense of coherence, that is, parataxis. It is characterized by more non-subject sentences and subject ellipsis sentences, with more active voice and comprehensive articles used, lack of conjunctions, and with no fear of repetition, balance and symmetry of words and sentences.

It is generally considered that thinking is common while language is national. Both language and way of thinking belong to the category of culture (its core is values), but they are also influenced by national culture and philosophy. Different social cultures have different values, and give birth to different nationalities. Different nationalities have different ways of thinking. Due to the differences in geography, history, culture and humanities, English and Chinese people have different values and different ways of thinking.

The Han nationality holds a mode of thinking based on intuition and sensibility, while the Western nation holds a mode of thinking based on logical straight-line reasoning. Tracing back to the origin of the differences in values and ways of thinking between English and Chinese, the physical and geographical conditions of ancient Chinese and Western societies have played a key role.

China is in a closed natural geographical environment on the mainland, which is less subject to pressure from nature. People pay attention to climate, geography and human harmony. This relaxed and harmonious atmosphere has helped Chinese people to shape the concept of "unity of man and nature" in ancient Chinese philosophy. This point of view contains two meanings: one is "the connection between man and nature", which refers to the universal laws and fundamental virtues of the universe and the human world, and which does not exist somewhere outside people, but is contained in people's own hearts, therefore the way of heaven is humanity, and vice versa.

The other is the theory of "similarity between heaven and man" put forward by Dong Zhongshu in the Han Dynasty, which holds that heaven and man are similar in physical nature. Whether it is "the connection between heaven and man" or "the similarity between man and nature", there is no obvious opposition between man and nature. People are used to understanding things as a whole and regard the world as an inseparable organism in nature. They tend to use this point of view to explain all things and phenomena. The Han nationality believes that the unity of opposites of *yin* and *yang* is the inherent attribute of objective things, such as heaven and earth, sun and moon in the universe, men and women in the world, and so on. It is the sympathetic action of *yin* and *yang* that causes the emergence, change and development of all things.

The ancestors of the Anglo-American nation lived in a marine environment with unrest and tough climate, which has formed the Anglo-American nation's emphasis on space expansion and military conquest, as well as a strong desire to conquer and conquer. Westerners divide the universe into two completely different worlds, which are opposite to each other, believing that everything in the world is opposite, such as man and nature, matter and spirit, society and nature, and so on. Man is considered to be separated from nature, who is in the position of dominating and transforming nature, striving for struggle. The constant conquest is a cosmological view of the separation of man and nature.

Different ways of life will inevitably have different material cultures, but also give rise to different values, beliefs, interests, behavioral habits, wisdom development direction and even psychology, with characters of a variety of

# Chapter Three  Chinese and English Cultural Thought Patterns

differences, as well as the formation of two completely different spiritual cultures. Chinese culture belongs to humanistic culture, while Western culture belongs to scientific culture. Humanistic culture emphasizes human theory and neglects artifacts. It emphasizes synthesis and neglects analysis. It also emphasizes understanding and neglects words and interpretation. On the contrary, scientific culture emphasizes material and neglects human theory. It emphasizes analysis and neglects synthesis. It also emphasizes concept and avoids generality.

Two different types of cultures have produced two different ways of thinking: the intuitive and perceptual mode of thinking of the Han nationality and the analytical and logical thinking mode of the Western nation. The characteristic of intuitive thinking is to grasp things as a whole, and the result of intuitive thinking is to emphasize the whole and ignore the individual. On the contrary, the Western nation's reflection of external things does not rely on intuitive understanding, but on the expression of abstract reason. The Western way of thinking is to decompose things into various components and analyze them in detail. The result of analytical thinking is to put individuals and parts in the first place.

After making a systematic comparison between Eastern and Western thinking, Suzuki and Fromm think that the Westerners' mind is analytical, individual, objective, universal, conceptual, systematic and so on. In contrast, the characteristics of Oriental thinking can be summarized as: comprehensive, integrated, subjective, unique, intuitive, non-systematic and so on. Mr. Fu Lei also said that there are basic differences in thinking between Easterners and Westerners. Easterners emphasize synthesis, re-induction, and implication while Westerners focus on analysis, subtle twists and turns, and description for fear of not being thorough.

The following are the details of the contrastive cultural thought patterns found in China and the West.

## 2. Synthesis VS Analysis (Synthetic/Holistic VS Analytic Thought Patterns)

### 2.1 Descriptions of Synthesis and Analysis

Synthesis means viewing an object in a way of combining in thought each part of the object as a whole with unification of its different nature, aspects, and relations (Kaplan, 1966). The synthetic thinking pattern emphasizes the overall understanding of nature and human society, that is, the whole concept and universality. This thought pattern is also called the holistic thinking.

Analysis means viewing an object in a way of decomposing in thought the whole object into each individual component, or differentiating its nature, aspects, and relations from each other (Kaplan, 1966). It dissects events and concepts into the pieces that can be linked in causal chains and categorized into universal criteria. Analytic thinking proceeds with relatively full awareness of the information and operations involved, the steps of which is explicit and usually can be adequately reported by the thinker to another individual. This kind of thinking stands in contrast to a more integrated approach, which is the holistic or synthetic one.

Synthesis and analysis are a unity of opposites. One can not reach the nature of an object and only stay on the surface if one is not in the position to decompose the object in parts. Similarly, if one can not view a thing by uniting its different components, one can not grasp the whole picture and can only result in a partial understanding. Therefore, synthesis and analysis interact and both weigh in the process of thinking.

In general, Chinese emphasize synthesis and Westerners stress analysis.

### 2.2 Chinese Thought pattern of Synthesis

Chinese emphasize perceiving and knowing things synthetically rather than analytically. In traditional Chinese philosophy, a holistic viewpoint of perceiving the world is highly esteemed.

## Chapter Three  Chinese and English Cultural Thought Patterns

In Chinese traditional philosophical systems, the universe is viewed as a vast, multidimensional, living organism consisting of many interdependent parts and forces, which constitute the entirety of the universe. This orientation tends to see the world as a unit — a world continuously creating and intimately infusing every aspect of the cosmos from its smallest detail to its grandest feature. Human beings in this orientation join body, mind, and spirit together.

Traditional CTP in China have been greatly influenced by such religious and philosophical systems as Confucianism, Taoism and Buddhism. The synthetic or holistic thinking is very much in accord with the view of Chinese philosophy presented in the *Book of Changes*, a classic in Chinese philosophy. The primary opposition of the *yin* and *yang* in the book is not viewed as one of antagonism but rather as one of complementarity. The *yin* is not complete without the *yang* and vice versa. The Chinese philosophy contains that it is impossible that one pole exists without the other. This holism has been expanded to cover the relations among objects in the world. It holds that heaven, earth and man are all viewed as a united whole.

Taoism advocates the idea of harmony of opposites, holding that the conflict is always comparatively superficial, for there can be no ultimate conflict when the pairs of objects are mutually interdependent.

Confucianism, largely a code of ethics governing human relationships, very rarely looks at the human individual simply as individual, but sees him as an integral part of the environment. Its concern is with order and harmony in family and society and not with the freedom of the individual (Zhang Zhongli and Zong Wenju, 2002).

Therefore, Chinese tend to synthesize elements into a unit, with the emphasis on the whole. They view the world as profoundly holistic. Therefore, this thinking pattern is also called holistic thinking. For thousands of years, this synthetic/holistic thinking pattern has occupied a dominant role in China and become the core of cognition and communication.

Under the influence of this holistic worldview, the Chinese also tend to observe things in their totality rather than to make careful analysis of each component. As a result, Chinese are used to making a survey of the overall situation first, and then thinking over details. This holistic priority causes the sequence of Chinese thinking process to be characterized as being from "whole" to "part", "large" to "small", "general" to "individual", "far" to "near", etc. In short, it is embodied in various facets of life in China.

**2.3　Western Thought Pattern of Analysis**

On the contrary, Westerners prefer analytic thinking to synthetic one. Traditional CTP in the West follow the Greek tradition. They are descended from the philosophers of ancient Greece and are shaped subsequently by Roman, Medieval European, and later Western thinkers.

Based on this philosophical system, Westerners stress analytic thinking patterns, which is the dominant pattern of thought in the West. They tend to analyze or dissect things into elements in order to understand them properly. They lay emphasis upon the parts rather than upon the whole of things and are quite strong and strict in classification and categorization. They perceive the world as being composed of separate pieces to be manipulated and examined. As a result, their emphasis is upon the parts rather than upon the whole of things. They tend to split an object into various parts for analysis rather than to take it as a whole for synthesis. For example, both Plato and Aristotle regarded definition and classification as essential tools for dealing with the nature of truth. This partial priority will undoubtedly lead to the sequence of Western thinking process to be characterized by being from "part" to "whole", "small" to "large", "individual" to 'general", "near" to "far", etc.

**2.4　Contrast of Synthesis and Analysis**

The contrast of sequences of thinking process caused by two different CTP is obviously reflected in the arrangement of the names, places and time

# Chapter Three  Chinese and English Cultural Thought Patterns

between China and the West. In China, the surname/family name descended from the ancestors of one's family is put in the first place. Then it is followed by the middle name if one has. It is given by one's family to show one's position in a family tree if one has a certain number of siblings or cousins. The last comes one's given name. For example, in Chinese names "侯耀文", and "侯耀华", "侯" is one's family name, "耀" is the middle name, and "文" "华" are the given names. Chinese names are typical examples that follow the sequence from "general" to "special", "family" to "individual".

Nevertheless, the order is totally reversed in the West. One's given name is usually placed at the beginning. Then follows one's middle name if one has any, which is sometimes one's father's given name. The last is one's family name. For example, in the name of the current American President "Joe Biden", "Joe" is a given name and "Biden" is the family name or called the surname. The similar situation appears in the arrangement of the places and time. Look at the following examples.

(1) We toured New York, one ① of the biggest cities ② in the world ③.

(1a) 我们去纽约旅行。纽约是世界上 ③ 最大的城市 ② 之一 ①。

(2) The current American president Joe Biden was born on 20 ① November ② (or November 20 in British English), 1942 ③.

(2a) 美国现任总统乔·拜登出生于 1942 ③ 年 11 ② 月 20 ①日。

(3) Early one morning ① in the summer ② of 2021 ③, three young men decided to go on a tour, they left the valley (1) of Jacksonville (2), in North Carolina (3), for the city of Charlotte.

(3a) 2021 ③ 年夏天 ② 的一个清晨 ①,三个年轻人决定去旅行。他们离开了北卡罗来纳州 (3) 的杰克逊维尔 (2) 村 (1),向夏洛特出发。

From the examples it is evident that in the West, organizing the places and time both follow the sequence from "small unit" to "large unit", as is shown in examples (1) (2) and (3), which is contrary to that in China as in (1a) (2a) and (3a). Specifically the order of the sequence arranged customarily in the West is like this: house number → street → district → county/city → province/state → country and the order of keeping time follows the sequence like: second → minute → hour → day → month → year. For instance, in sentence (1), "one" comes before "the biggest cities" and "the biggest cities" comes before "the world" in English and the reverse is true in Chinese as is shown in (1a) as "世界上最大的城市之一".

The sequence of ranging from smaller unit to larger unit is the reflection of partial priority of analytic thinking stressing on "part" more than "whole" in the expression of English. And the reverse sequence reflects the holistic thinking in the expression of Chinese.

Another example that can reflect these thought patterns is the Chinese characters and the English words. It is known that Chinese characters include three dimensions: ideogram (signs representing the meaning), phonogram (signs representing the sound) and pictogram (signs representing the form). A Chinese character is often considered from those three angles, which contributes to the development of synthetic thought pattern.

Conversely, English words are one-dimension words considered from one single aspect of phonogram, which promotes the development of analytical thought pattern.

## 3. Unity VS Dichotomy/Dualism (Unitive VS Dichotomous/Dualistic Thinking)

### 3.1 Chinese Thought Pattern of Unity

Chinese accent harmony and infiltration between the two opposites, that is, unity in opposition. They emphasize that all differences are relative within

Chapter Three   Chinese and English Cultural Thought Patterns

an encompassing phenomenon. All opposites are interactive and interdependent; their conflict can never result in the total victory of one side but will always be a manifestation of the interplay between the two sides. They realize that good and bad, pleasure and pain, life and death, winning and losing, light and dark, are not absolute experiences belonging to different categories, but merely two sides of the same reality — extreme parts of a single continuum.

So Chinese thinking is strongly relational and strives for unity between events or objects. The four major schools of Chinese philosophy — Confucianism, Taoism, the Yin-yang School, and Chinese Buddhism contribute to the thought of unity. Throughout history these four schools have been paralleling and reinforcing each other. The central concerns of Confucianism are the harmonious universe and the superior man. It also suggests centrality and harmony. In general, the thought of unity is definitely revealed in the Confucian system.

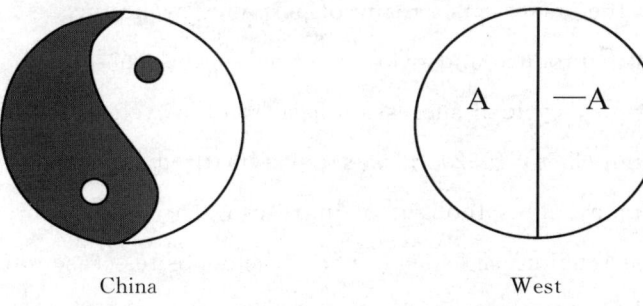

Figure 1

This thought is strengthened as the Yin-yang School established by Tung Chung-shu, who combines the Confucian doctrines of ethics with the idea of Yin and Yang, stating that all things had their complements in Yin and Yang. No aspect of Chinese civilization has escaped the imprint of the Yin-yang School's doctrines. Yin stands for being negative, cold, downward and inward, dark, and night, which also represents being feminine. Yang stands for being positive, hot, upward and outward, light, and day, which also represents being masculine. As is shown in the diagram on the left in figure 1, the Yin and Yang interact with each other. Where one grows, the other contracts, but they make a whole. Neither can exist independently without the other. Furthermore, each has an element of the other within it. As the Yin grows larger, so does the Yang element within it, and vice-versa.

This concept of harmony and infiltration between the two opposites is later succeeded by the concept of the five elements: water to moisten and descend; fire to flame and ascend; wood, to straighten and to be crooked; metal, to yield and to be modified; and soil, to provide for sowing and reaping. When these five elements in each category come fully and in their regular order, all living things will be rich and luxuriant. If there is extreme excess in any one, disaster will follow.

The Yin-yang Confucianism dominates Chinese thought for five centuries. It maintains that multiplicity rises from the constant interaction of Yin and Yang and that the universe is a realm of perpetual cyclic succession of the Five Elements, which produce and overcome one another in a fixed sequence and that the history is a cycle of succession based on the cycle of the Five Elements (Robert Shanmu Chen, 1992). It was a systematized expression of the idea of unity and harmony. This thought of unity can also be discovered in another ancient Chinese religion — Taoism. That "the opposites cease to be opposites" (Young Yun Kim, 1994) is the very essence of Taoism, which holds that the opposites are relative and temporary whereas the unity is absolute, permanent and everlasting.

One of Taoism's representatives, Chuang Tzu conceives that the universe is the unity of all things. He says "if we attain this unity and identify ourselves with it, then the members of our body are but so much dust and dirt, while life and death, end and beginning, are but as the succession of day and night, which cannot disturb our inner peace" (Fung Yu-lan, 1997: 114-115).

# Chapter Three   Chinese and English Cultural Thought Patterns

Although these schools differ in details of their doctrines, the general conceptions keep the same. They interact with each other and eventually form the Chinese thought pattern of unity.

## 3.2  Western Theought Pattern of Dualism

Totally different from Chinese thought, westerners possess the dichotomous thought. Where the western view is dualistic, the eastern view is profoundly nondualistic. The Westerners often perceive the world as being composed of separate pieces to be manipulated and examined.

Specifically, they accent struggle and transformation between the two opposites, that is, opposition in unity. They struggle to eliminate one of a pair of opposites in favor of the other. Specifically, they are accustomed to seeing the world in terms of dichotomies and separating everything into two opposites, such as work VS play, good VS bad/evil, war VS peace, right VS wrong, beautiful VS ugly, success VS failure, man VS nature, God VS humankind, mind VS body, etc (Stewart, 1985). This kind of thought pattern is a common Indo-European thinking, which stems from ancient Greece, where Plato and his school conveniently distinguished matter from ideas, and the soma (body) from the psyche (mind).

This oppositional thinking leads Westerners to a simplified recognition of the world as either black or white. They view the two parts totally separated and diametrically opposed, i.e., things just have two possibilities, either this or that, as is revealed in the diagram on the right in figure 1. If it is "A", it can't be "-A". While if it is "not A", it must be "-A". This point of view of dichotomizing the things is what is called dichotomy or dualism. Based on this concept, Westerners usually jump to a conclusion about everything by this standard, which is considered a rude behavior in the East.

The core of western cultural values represented by the United States is individualism. Its main content is to believe in personal value, attaching great importance to individual freedom, and emphasizing personal self-domination, self-control and self-development, which is the individual-based philosophy of life. Samwa, an American scholar, further explained that the values of individualism in American culture include independent motivation, independent choice, self-reliance, respect for others, individual freedom, respect for privacy and so on.

### 3.3 Contrast of Chinese Collectivism and Western Individualism

Western scholars point out that "individualism" and "egoism" are two different concepts. Tocqueville said that egoism is an extreme excessive love for oneself, which makes people only care about themselves and love themselves more than anything else. Egoism is an emotion that only cares for itself and is at ease. It isolates every citizen from the masses of his compatriots and from relatives and friends. It can be seen that the individualism in American mind is different from the interpretation of this concept in Cihai. Americans are adventurous. The Guinness Book of World Records holders are mostly Americans who have something to do with this.

This is contrary to Chinese traditional culture. There is such a famous saying in the ancient Chinese: "If the wood is better than the forest, the wind will destroy it; if you act above the masses, you must be wrong." There are also some sayings such as "shooting a bird with a gun" "a big tree attracts the wind" and so on. For example, in class, American students like to sit in front and raise their hands when answering questions, while Chinese students like to sit back and wait and be ready to answer questions raised by the teachers.

In contrast to American individualistic values, there is collectivism in Chinese tradition, and some people call it familism and magnified family values. In the relationship between the individual and the collective, it is stressed that the interests of the collective are always higher than those of the individual. Individual interests should be integrated into collective interests and, if necessary, sacrifice individual interests and obey collective interests. It emphasizes man's obligation and responsibility to society. Individual honor,

## Chapter Three  Chinese and English Cultural Thought Patterns

disgrace and success are closely linked with the collective.

In Chinese, there are sayings like "to make one's ancestors illustrious" "to worry before the people worry, and be happy only after the people are happy" "the world is shared by the people" "win glory for the country" and so on. Words like these are the embodiment of this concept of collectivism.

Of course, Chinese cultural tradition also believes that individuals should have personality, personal beliefs, personal interests and pursuit, but they are not supposed to put them above society. Personal value and social responsibility are unified. This is also an important factor in the strong cohesion of the Chinese nation. For example, Chinese athletes show an outstanding spirit of collectivism in the sports world.

However, from another point of view, too much emphasis on "collective" can easily lead to the neglect of individual rights and freedoms, and affect the development of personality and the development of individual autonomy and creativity, which can be clearly found from the previous comparison with American individualistic values. Conversely, with too much emphasis on "personality", it is sometimes easy to lead to apathy in interpersonal relationships, family indifference, and even alcohol and drug abuse to vent mental depression and loneliness.

The mode of thinking of Chinese culture is rooted in the simple understanding of nature, which is observed as a whole according to the true nature of nature. Man and nature, as well as individual and society are inseparable, which influence each other and correspond to each other. It is suggested to put everything in the relationship of network and comprehensively examine its organic relationship as a whole. This kind of holistic thinking is also called comprehensive thinking.

Conversely, western culture emphasizes thinking according to a certain procedure, deducing the unknown from the known, demonstrating meticulously like analytical geometry, and then drawing logical conclusions.

This method of dividing the object into various parts in thinking activities and studying them one by one is the characteristic of analytical thinking.

The Chinese prefer comprehensiveness, which leads to the overall priority in thinking. This way of thinking from the whole to the part is also reflected in the expression of language, such as the expression and order of time is from big to small, from year to month, and then to day, week, hour, minute and second; the narrative order of spatial position is also from big to small, from country to province, city, district, street and house number. When characters are introduced, their titles appear first and their positions are introduced step by step from big to small, and lastly appear their names.

Furthermore, the British and Americans express it in the opposite way. In English it is habitually ranged from small to large, and from minor content to main content, which is the embodiment of Westerners' way of thinking from the part to the whole in their languages.

## 4. Subjective Consciousness VS Objective Consciousness

### 4.1 Chinese Thought Pattern of Subjoctive Consciousness

Chinese tend to unite the objective world (the natural world) with the subjective world (the perceiver of the natural world, namely the animate things esp. human beings) and somewhat value more of the latter. This orientation is reflected in traditional Chinese culture, in which unity of nature and human beings is the ideal state and they are regarded as a whole. Harmony between man and nature becomes the highest standard for man's self-cultivation.

Chinese celebrate wilderness and preserve an image more integrated with nature. Human beings are just another form of the physical world, not in opposition to it. All forms of life and inanimate objects are considered to be the unity. This thought can also be certified by the Chinese traditional philosophical schools, all of which, on the whole, are apt to mixing the two.

## Chapter Three  Chinese and English Cultural Thought Patterns

Confucianism is always a humanism that professes a harmonious universe, and the unity of man and cosmos.

In Chinese "Jen", which means benevolence, is human nature and righteousness or justice, and the Confucian "Jen" includes not only all human beings but also the universe in its totality. In this connection "Jen" is expanded to the concept of integration with the universe, the mind or heart of humans, the foundation of all goodness, the generative force of all things and the source of all production in the universe.

Ancient thinker Mencius said that he who exerts his mind to the utmost knows his nature; he who knows his nature knows Heaven. The Yin-yang school argues that there is mutual influence between Man and Nature. Taoism also states the harmony of man with nature. Zhuangzhi also remarked that Heaven and Earth come into being with me together, and to me, all things are one.

Chinese Buddhism, another important religion evolved from India, believes in the identification of man with the universal mind. In general, traditional Chinese culture regards human beings and nature as a whole and values harmony between human beings and harmony between man and nature. Such a belief in "harmony between nature and man" gives rise to a strong personal consciousness of the Chinese people in expressing their ideas. So, the object (the world) and the subject (the perceiver of the world) are never strictly split, which are always mixed together. In Chinese grammar the frequent omission of subjects reflects the mixture and harmony of human beings and nature.

Furthermore, in ancient China, it is considered that human beings are the center of the cosmos. Chinese people value human beings more than the natural world, which also contributes to the subjective consciousness in Chinese. In short, Chinese tend to mix the subject and the object of the world and at the same time stress subjective consciousness or personal consciousness with the observation of the world from the point of view of human beings or "animate" things, which is opposite of the objective consciousness in the West.

**4.2　Western Thought Pattern of Objective Consciousness**

In the West, the separation between man and nature survives and remains securely in place to this day. The division between human and nature and the bias against the wilderness has a long tradition in the western world. Western philosophy, advocating logical and rational analysis, premises keeping the distance between subject and object in order to dissect things objectively and soberheadedly.

Moreover, dichotomous thinking influences Westerners so much that they hold men and nature exist in opposition, so they study the cosmos as an object and regard nature as an opposition and something to conquer. They consider nature to be the cognitive object for human beings. The nature, namely the whole cosmos is completely incompatible with human beings. Consequently, Westerners strictly set apart subjective world from objective one.

At the same time in the West, people have conceived the universe as having been initially created and, since then, externally controlled by a Divine power. As such, the western worldview is characteristically dualistic, materialistic, and lifeless.

The Judeo-Christian tradition sets "God" apart from this reality. Having created it and set it into motion, God is viewed as apart from "His" creation. The fundamental material of the universe is conceived to be essentially nonliving matter, or elementary particles of matter. "It is as though the universe is an inanimate machine wherein humankind occupies a unique and elevated position among the life forms that exist. Assuming a relatively barren universe, it seems only rational that humans make use of the lifeless material universe on behalf of the most intensely living — humankind itself." (Linda Beamer & Iris Varner, 2000: 432)

The Western view of nature has led to objectivity about the world and the development of science and technology. As a result, the Westerners conceive the objectivity of the world with the consideration of dichotomizing the subjective world and the objective one and it seems they value more of the latter.

## 4.3 Contrast of Chinese Subjective Consciousness and Western Objective Consciousness

Chinese traditional thinking emphasizes being people-oriented, regarding itself as the center of the universe, and believing that the inner experience is the starting point of all cognition. This kind of thinking tends to focus on inward exploration, that is, to know and perfect oneself, but this introversion does not highlight the independent status of the individual. On the contrary, the group includes the individual, will naturally contain in the hearts of the people, with man as the heaven and the unity of man and nature to feel and understand all things through the integration of subject and object. This forms the subjective thinking of the Han nationality.

Subjective thinking often points to itself, seeking harmony between man and nature, taking people as the center when observing things, and accustomed to narrating objective things from the self when narrating events or stating viewpoints. It tends to describe people and their behavior or state. Therefore, the personal subject is often used in Chinese, that is, words that represent people or creatures are used as subjects. This also leads to the frequent use of active voice in Chinese.

Different from the Chinese subjective consciousness, the western traditional thinking takes nature as the cognitive object, and holds that only by understanding nature can people grasp nature, and only by exploring nature can they conquer nature, so there is a dichotomy between subject and object, and the opposition between heaven and man. It divides the inner world from the external nature, and distinguishes between self-consciousness and cognitive objects. Therefore, Westerners attach importance to the natural object, emphasizing the existence of the object. The goal of thinking often points to the outside world.

Under the influence of this consciousness, objective thinking is formed, and the objective world is regarded as the object of observation, analysis and research. Reflected in language, English is often referred to as the subject with non-biological or abstract concepts, paying attention to the role and influence of things on people, so that things are presented in an objective tone.

## 5.Intuition VS Logic

### 5.1 Chinese Thought Pattern of Intuition

Intuition is a straightforward and immediate process of comprehending suddenly and thoroughly instead of a process of advancing gradually from "part" to "whole". It does not advance in careful, well-defined steps. Indeed, it tends to be based on seemingly implicit perception of the total problem. The thinker arrives at an answer with little if any awareness of the process by which he reaches it. Intuition transcends the data of the senses and the manipulation of the mind to perceive truths that seem to lie beyond reason, according to Fisher and Luyster (1991). They hold that intuitive wisdom can not be verified by the senses or the scientific instruments that we use to extend the range of perception. It emerges into awareness in an entirely different way than does logical thought.

As Chinese recognize the world from the point of view of entirety instead of practical analysis, they tend to perceive it from intuition. Fisher and Luyster (1991) observe that eastern approaches have developed meditation techniques that encourage intuitive wisdom to rise from the depths — or the voice of the divine to descend into individual consciousness. Among traditional ancient Chinese religions, Confucianism, Taoism and Chinese Buddhism, regardless of their dissimilation, all suggest understanding the objects by insightful intuition. Chinese signify an emphasis on direct experiences, and tend to stick to empiricism in theory. Therefore, they achieve intuitive comprehension and insight, which is very difficult to explain in words, only to be sensed by the mind and does not allow people to understand an object very clearly. It stresses on the direct and immediate apprehension of the "whole" in a twinkling, which always causes the ambiguity.

For instance, in Chinese traditional religions, concepts like "天""道" "气""理" are quite ambiguous and unclear. In Chinese there are sentences without subjects or predicates as they are not the indispensable parts. For example, sentences like "下雨了""太晚了""8点了" don't possess the subjects and others like "天高云淡""山穷水尽" don't contain the predicates.

This kind of intuitive thinking holds that one does not find the truth by active searching and the application of Aristotelian modes of reasoning; on the contrary, one just waits and keeps patient, and if truth is to be known it will make itself apparent. In this way of thinking, the Chinese have considered intuitive insight as the superior means of perceiving truth. They do not show too much interest in the precise details of factual events, but see them as a whole and rely heavily on all the contextual cues in a communication transaction. A more typical instance is the Chinese ancient poetry, most of which are apparently implicit and vague. The implication and the metaphoric meaning of them are to be left to the readers themselves to comprehend. Here is a Chinese poem by Meng Haoran, named "The Spring Dawn"(《春晓》).

春眠不觉晓, Slumbering, I know not the spring dawn is peeping,
处处闻啼鸟。but everywhere the singing birds are cheeping.
夜来风雨声, Last night I heard the rain dripping and wind weeping,
花落知多少。how many petals are now on the ground sleeping?

This Chinese poem is a very famous one among poems in Tang Dynasty, which becomes household word with its plain, vivid, natural and graceful utterance. It is complete in structure but no any connective functional word is applied, which seems superficially ambiguous and lack of concentration in meaning to western readers. Throughout the whole passage the subject is omitted without stating who is slumbering in the spring (春眠), who hears the birds cheeping (闻啼鸟), the rain dripping and the wind weeping (风雨声).

While the omission of the subject won't hamper the understanding of the poem because the readers — Chinese possess and are accustomed to the intuitive thought. However, when such a poem is translated into English, the English customary rules of sentence structures have to be taken into account. Therefore, the subject "I" ought to be added to the original sentences as is shown in the previous translation by Wu Juntao. At the same time, as it stresses the power of understanding and intuitional experience, this thinking pattern will certainly cause the comprehension of the meanings by perception and insightful intuition. Therefore, the meanings are to be sensed and realized without stating clearly or using noticeable connectors, which usually brings the ambiguity of meanings and leads to a striking characteristic in Chinese, namely, parataxis.

### 5.2 Western Thought Pattern of Logic

Logical thinking is the thinking activity governed by the rules of Aristotle's logic, which uses the systematic and theoretical elaboration while dealing with an issue and emphasizes the logical analysis and dissection, dissecting an object into separate parts and analyzing them respectively (Kaplan, 1966). It stresses the completeness of the structure and the strictness of the form, involving careful and deductive reasoning, or it may involve a step-by-step process of induction and experiment, utilizing principles of research design and statistical analysis.

European and North American cultures have a system of logic based on

# Chapter Three  Chinese and English Cultural Thought Patterns

Aristotle's theory, which is reflected by the westerners' thinking pattern. Westerners prefer analytical thinking, recognizing the nature of the objects by means of logical analysis, which may involve careful and deductive reasoning. The syllogism has served as the cornerstone of the western thinking pattern for about 2500 years. Westerners believe that truth is out there and that they can discover it only by following scientific methods and engaging in logical calculations. Therefore, they are quite strong in classification and categorization.

Greek philosopher Plato and Aristotle regarded definition and classification as essential tools for dealing with the nature of truth. As a result, English is characterized as precise, strict, and meticulous. For example, in "*Dream of the Red Chamber*", the sentences like "你死了，我去当和尚" are the typical ones reflecting the Chinese intuitional thought. If it is translated into English, some words are necessary to be added to show the relations and the tense. So, the suggested one is "<u>If</u> you were dead, I <u>would</u> be a monk."

In English the subjects and objects are clearly divided, which are two indispensable parts in sentences except for the imperative ones. So, the subjects that are usually omitted in Chinese have to be added to the sentences when put into English except in elliptical ones. If there is no any clear subject in a sentence, a formal subject "it" should be added to serve the function, such as "<u>It</u> is raining." "<u>It</u> was too late." "<u>It</u>'s 8 o'clock", etc. The completeness and strictness lead to hypotaxis in English. Parataxis and hypotaxis are two major characteristics in language organization, which will be discussed in detail in the next chapter.

## 5.3  Contrast of Intuition and Logic

Chinese people are used to thinking in images, paying more attention to intuitive experience in the process of understanding the world, and carrying out analogical analysis on the basis of feeling, perception and representation.

With the help of intuitive experience, this kind of thinking grasps the inner essence and law of the cognitive object directly and vaguely through perception.

Westerners are used to abstract thinking and reflect objective reality with the help of concepts, judgment, reasoning and other forms of thinking in the process of cognition. It uses scientific abstract concepts and categories to reveal the nature of things. Because this process is carried out in accordance with logical laws, it is also called logical thinking. The abstract logical thinking of Westerners has a strong color of demonstration, rationality and speculation.

Chinese people prefer image thinking, while European and American people prefer abstract logical thinking, which is also reflected in Chinese and English languages, especially in the characters and words used in Chinese and English. The outstanding feature of Chinese characters is that the glyph structure can reflect the meaning of the word in varying degrees, that is, it can be "shaped into meaning".

Chinese characters, originated from pictures, is a kind of pictographic characters, and have gradually developed into pictographs. Although its pictographic features have declined a lot after thousands of years of evolution and simplification, some Chinese characters still have pictographic features, such as:"人、山、川、水、口、凹、凸、伞" and so on. Most of the characters in modern Chinese are pictophonetic characters, in which the meaning beside the form is the signifier and the phonetic symbol is the phonetic symbol with both the representation of the sound and the meaning, through which the text is vivid. For example, the words used as signifiers beside "手" are mostly related to the actions of the hand, such as "拉、扯、推、按" and so on, in which "立、止、佳、安" is for pronunciation. From the perspective of word formation, Chinese is also accustomed to using figurative metaphors, which make people have intuitive and vivid associations, such as"漆黑——像漆那样黑;金贵——像金子那样贵重;火热——像火一样热"。

# Chapter Three  Chinese and English Cultural Thought Patterns

It can be seen that Chinese is in line with the habit of thinking in images of the Chinese people, which can make people have an image and intuitive association. Compared with Chinese characters of phonetic writing, in Europe and the United States alphabetic writing is used without the expression of meaning. The initial selection of letters is also random, and there is no inevitable relationship between pronunciation and the correspondent symbols of letters. For example, which pronunciations are expressed by symbols such as the letters "a, b, c and d" and so on are all established at first, then they gradually develop into a kind of symbols, and finally a connection between sound and meaning is formed. Whereas phonetic characters determine the meaning by combination of the sound, which leads to the signaling and logicalization of the language.

People in the West are good at abstract thinking, which is reflected in a whole set of ways to express abstract thinking in the language, such as the extensive use of abstract nouns in sentences. These abstract nouns have a general meaning and general reference, and are easy to express complex thoughts and subtle emotions. Most of these nouns are transformed from other parts of speech by means of falsification, that is, adding affixes, especially suffixes, etc., such as suffixes for status like "-ness" "-tion" "-ity" "-ence" "-hood" and so on. For many English abstract nouns, the corresponding parts of speech can not be found in Chinese dictionaries, such as absence, carelessness, youth, sensation, honesty, motherhood and so on. In addition, there are many English prepositions, which can express vague and abstract meanings.

The Han nationality is sensitive to image thinking, and Chinese tends to turn the abstract into concrete, often expressing the virtual concept in the real form and expressing the abstract content in the concrete image. Therefore, it is often possible to materialize and visualize the meaning of abstract concepts when English is translated into Chinese. While Chinese is put into English, the specific content can be abstracted.

For example, "lack of perseverance" is translated as "三天打鱼,两天晒网", and "perfect harmony" is translated into "水乳交融" and so on. From the examples it is obvious that English abstract expressions are translated into Chinese concrete images. On the contrary, the Chinese idiom "种瓜得瓜,种豆得豆" can be translated as "As you sow, you will reap." There is no need to rack one's brains to try to translate specific things like "瓜" and "豆" into English.

The characteristics of English and Chinese sentence structures are consistent with the characteristics of the way of thinking. In Chinese, sentences are arranged with the method of ordering, and the word order can be compared with the order in which human beings perceive the world, which also reflects the Chinese way of thinking that the outside world is known by intuition and perception. The technique of construction is used in English sentences, through which the predicate verb is taken as the axis and all kinds of words are used to express the formal relations to embed each component of the sentence before and after the two main trunks of the subject and predicate, showing a spatial schema extending outward from the central word to build a spatial framework.

English is seen as a sort of analytical language. Sentence structure reflects the western nation's reflection of external things, which does not rely on intuitive perceptual knowledge but on abstract rational expression. It is with a kind of analytical and logical thinking mode. From the logical point of view of English writing, the effect comes first and the cause comes later, which fully embodies the characteristics of the analytical and logical mode of thinking. It is often reflected in the language that in Chinese the cause is talked about first, then follows the effect. It emphasizes a specific or objective reason to produce the result. Comparatively, in English effect or result often comes first and then follows the cause.

# Chapter Three  Chinese and English Cultural Thought Patterns

For example, when writing a letter to borrow some valuables from a friend, a Chinese usually mentions a lot of irrelevant words in a circle before revealing the real purpose. The length of the article often makes Westerners lose the patience to read on because they don't know what the author is going to say. The practice of people from English-speaking countries is on the contrary. After a few pleasantries, they come straight to the point and don't beat around the bush.

Mr. Hu Wenzhong and others compare the writing style of English articles tobeing "linear", that is, each paragraph begins with a topic sentence, followed by an example sentence, and ends with an example sentence, or ends with a topic sentence.

In contrast, the way of writing in Chinese is being "spiral", that is, it does not directly demonstrate the theme of the paragraph, but indirectly demonstrates the theme from various peripheral angles. These differences are consistent with the differences in thinking patterns between English and Chinese.

## 6.Imagination and Concreteness VS Abstraction

### 6.1  Descriptions of Imagery Thinking and Abstract Thinking

Imagery thinking refers to the psychological process of analyzing, synthesizing and processing the memorized images in one's mind and finally forming new images, that is, the imagination of material concepts (Kaplan, 1966). It is a basic type of thinking whereby the thinker uses some highly concrete forms, which are readily apprehended by themselves, to express the meanings of some concepts.

Abstract thinking is the thinking activity of judging and reasoning with abstract concepts (Kaplan, 1966). It is characterized by the thinker's employment of some notions including models, theories, classifications and so on.

## 6.2 Chinese Thought Pattern of Imagination

Chinese have preference for imagination, namely, imagery thinking. It has been observed that one of the most important characteristics of Chinese psychology is its reliance on sense and perception. Chinese people emphasize direct perception, in particular visual perception, of the world. Concrete objects that are directly sensible or visually noticeable are often in the first place to be observed. It is through perception, not analytical thinking nor scientific reasoning that Chinese people acquire the initial knowledge of the environment they are living in. Some even claim that the Chinese are reluctant to dwell on that which is beyond the immediate perception. Consequently, the Chinese tend to see abstract and general aspects in terms of the concrete and particular ones.

The Chinese imagination is reflected remarkably in the way in which the Chinese characters are made. Different from English letters that are alphabetic ones, the Chinese characters are hieroglyphics or ideograms, which, in their earliest forms, were pictures of things or ideas and gradually developed into symbols. Symbolism is the characteristic of Chinese characters.

For example, the ancient Chinese character "⊙", which represents the sun, seems apparently like the image of the sun. Even in modern Chinese characters, with the evolution and development of language, some still keep the attribute of imagination. Take modern Chinese characters "日" "水" "田" "凹" and "凸" as the examples, which stand for the "sun" "water" "field" "concave" and "convex" respectively. The original shapes of these characters are based on the shapes of the natural objects.

Although modern Chinese characters are not a system of picture writing, they still use some complex means to convey ideas vividly with images. For example, "从" is a vivid description of a man following the other. "雨" has four dot strokes symbolizing raindrops.

In addition, Chinese imagery thinking is so deeply rooted in Chinese

# Chapter Three  Chinese and English Cultural Thought Patterns

culture that it has continued to exert its influence on Chinese literature, as can be proved by analogy. Chinese widely use the method of imagery analogy and express their ideas through images of objects. In traditional Chinese literary works, the figures of using imagination frequently appear while the abstraction doesn't comparatively develop so well. There are many examples of words and expressions in Chinese, which are very concrete and vivid creating corresponding images in people's mind at sight to represent common things or rather abstract implication. Look at the following examples in Chinese:

百褶裙 (pleated skirt, a skirt with seemingly a hundred pleats on it);

灯笼袖 (puffed sleeve, the sleeve seemed to be puffed just like a lantern);

马蹄铁 (horseshoe, whose shape seems like a horse's hoof);

回形针 (paper clip, a clip used to hold things together with several curves);

蚕食 (means "to nibble, just like a silkworm eating the mulberry leaves");

失之交臂 (means "just miss the person or opportunity, implying being so close to each other that their arms almost touch");

如日中天 (means "at the apex of one's power, career, etc. just like the sun at high noon").

## 6.3 Western Thought Pattern of Abstraction

In contrast, Westerners value abstract thinking. This thought pattern is reflected by the wide use of abstract nouns in English. The meanings of these nouns are quite general, abstract and seemingly vague. They are often used to express complex ideas and subtle emotions. For example, in the sentence "Comparable statistics are the basis of a single monetary policy." "statistics" is a fairly abstract noun, which, in Chinese, is expressed more concrete as "统计表". Another example is "Little was heard of him in the next few years." "Little" here is an abstract noun representing "very few things or nearly nothing".

Moreover, in English, large numbers of suffixes that possess abstract meanings such as "-ness" "-ship" "-hood", etc. are applied to compose the abstract nouns. Besides, the wide use of prepositions is another example to show the abstractness in English. For example, "A motorcycle is beyond my reach." Here a preposition "beyond" is used instead of using the verb "buy" as in the sentence "I can not afford to buy a motorcycle."

## 7. Indirectness VS Directness in the Process of Expressing Ideas

### 7.1 Chinese Thought Pattern of Indirectness

As it is mentioned previously, in China, Confucianism, Taoism, and Buddhism, which have great influence on Chinese society, all pursue intuition, that is, the power of understanding the meaning between the lines. Therefore, Chinese people tend to use an indirect way of expressing their opinions or use an ambiguous statement. Besides, as a result of emphasis on imagery and concrete thought, Chinese people are inclined to make judgments based on the events that occurred before, or precedent, in other words, the Chinese believe that something happened with a precedent to refer to is more valid and trustworthy.

Furthermore, Chinese tradition emphasizes collective power and collectivism. It does not allow for much individual self-expression. The position, function and opinion of an individual have always been reduced. All these factors lead to the indirectness in Chinese thought. Such a mentality is traceable in the Chinese people's attitude towards the *Four Books* and *Five Classics*. The *Four Books* and *Five Classics* have been works of the highest authority regarded as providing the norms for human life throughout the Chinese history.

In the Analects of Confucius, actions of individuals and the dicta of Confucius are recorded, which are used to enlighten people that the way to be a perfect gentleman is to live in a manner as the Great Thinker thought it should be. Confucius once said in his Analects, "I do not invent, but merely transmit; I believe in and love antiquity." and "I am not a man born wise. I favor what is ancient and strive to know it well." For him, learning implies full knowledge of the precedents of a past age.

Under such instruction, the Chinese also try to discover in precedents the laws governing life. Such kind of thought pattern is reflected in the abundance of literary and historical allusions in Chinese texts. The Chinese attach great importance to expressions based on historical particularity, as they believe these expressions will help add a flavor of authority to their sayings or articles. As a result, Chinese people who aim at pointing out their opinions seldom operate it directly and straightforwardly but always quote predecessors' and celebrities' remarks.

**7.2 Western Thought Pattern of Directness**

In the West, the ideas of Ancient Greek philosophers like Socrates, Plato and Aristotle have great influence upon the society. They advocate logic and reasoning. In addition, individual's point of view is emphasized in the history of the whole Western society. As a result, Western people are encouraged to express their opinions directly. The English cultural preference is for clear and direct communication as evidence by many common English expressions. For instance, "Say what you mean." "Don't beat around the bush." and "Get to the point." In general, English contains linearity and directness in expression.

Mode of thinking is a kind of thinking form in which human beings solidify their understanding of objective reality into experience and habits, form ideas with the help of language, and endow them with certain patterns in the long process of history. Different nations not only have different national cultures, but also have their own distinctive ways of thinking, thinking characteristics and thinking styles, which is the thinking diversity. The difference in thinking reflects the psychological tendency of the language formed by the ethnic groups of a certain language for thousands of years.

### 7.3 Contrast of Indirectness and Directness

There is a great difference in the way of thinking between English and Chinese, which is closely related to the physical and geographical conditions, social and cultural background of the English and Chinese people. Due to the different natural and geographical environments, English and Chinese people have formed their own national cultural atmosphere and distinctive cultural way of thinking.

China is located in the Asian continent and develops in a closed geographical environment. Due to less pressure from nature, people pay attention to the right time, geographical location and harmony. They gradually formed the philosophical view of the unity of man and nature, which tends to regard the world as an indivisible organic whole and is used to understanding things as a whole.

The Anglo-American nation is located in an oceanic climate, frequently affected by severe weather and climate, which gradually formed their strong desire to conquer and control by paying attention to space expansion and conquering others by force. At the same time, it has gradually formed the unique cosmology and world outlook of Westerners, that is, dividing the universe into two completely different worlds, believing that everything in the world is opposite, emphasizing the opposition between heaven and earth, man and nature, matter and spirit, society and nature. They advocate the separation of heaven and man, and the two are opposed to each other. Man is separated from nature, man is in the position of dominating and transforming nature, striving for struggle and constant conquest is a cosmological view of the separation of man and nature.

Different ways of life form different world views and cosmology, and it is bound to form different material cultures, but also give rise to different values, beliefs and interests. From the perspective of cultural origin, Chinese

## Chapter Three　Chinese and English Cultural Thought Patterns

culture has a long history for thousands of years and Buddhism is the only foreign factor in the broad and profound Chinese traditional culture.

There are three main sources of western culture: Greek culture, Jewish culture and modern industrialism. Western culture is formed by the confluence of many kinds of national cultures. The economic basis of the emergence and development of Chinese traditional culture is agricultural economy, which possesses the characteristics of strong closeness and introversion, and which pursues the unity of man and nature and conforms to nature. All these make Chinese traditional culture embark on the road of introspection and internal pursuit from the date of its birth. The economic basis of the emergence and development of Western culture is commodity economy, which is characterized by the exchange of needed goods. The European culture produced on this economic basis has the characteristics of extroversion and openness.

The way of thinking produced under different cultural backgrounds will naturally be influenced by their own cultural traditions, showing completely different characteristics of thinking.

English and Chinese have different geographical environments and cultural backgrounds, which have formed very different cultural thinking patterns. Thinking to some degree dominates language and is expressed through language. In the process of language transmission, its content and form are marked with the mode of thinking. Therefore, the information transmitted by a certain language is easy to be understood by people who are influenced by the same or similar cultural mode of thinking, while people affected by different cultural modes of thinking sometimes find it difficult to understand or even misunderstand. It can be clearly seen that the influence of way of thinking on spoken and written language can not be ignored.

# Chapter Four
# The Reflection of CTP in Chinese and English Languages

Since culture, thought and language closely are related to and interact with each other, the cultural thought patterns as the backbone of the culture have found their way into the language. Chinese and English languages are inevitably influenced by their respective cultural thought patterns. In this part, six aspects of most distinct contrastive phenomena in the two languages influenced by the cultural thought patterns are studied and compared.

## 1.Parataxis VS Hypotaxis

### 1.1 Causes of Chinese Preference in Parataxis and English Preference in Hypotaxis

Parataxis refers to the arrangement of clauses following the characteristics of one after another without connectives showing the relation between them, as in the example "The rain fell; the river flooded; the house washed away", according to the *World Book Dictionary*.

Hypotaxis indicates the dependent or subordinate construction or relationship of clauses with connectives, for example, "I shall despair if you don't come." according to the *American Heritage Dictionary*.

Parataxis and hypotaxis coexist in both Chinese and English, but Chinese is more paratactic and English is more hypotactic. The synthetic, unitive, intuitive and subjective consciousness thoughts in China and the analytical,

# Chapter Four  The Reflection of CTP in Chinese and English Languages

logical, and objective consciousness thoughts in the West contribute to the parataxis in Chinese and the hypotaxis in English.

As the synthetic thought pursues the unity and harmony of the "part" and the "whole", requiring the understanding of things as a whole, it employs synthesis in observing things and stresses the intuition in comprehension. Consequently, it develops the emphasis on the sense and meaning and at the same time neglects the formal logic, which reflects the paratactic preference in Chinese language, namely, valuing the integrity and completeness in content and meaning.

Conversely, analytical and logic thought stresses logical analysis and individual independence, based on experience and emphasizing formal logic and reasoning, which, correspondingly causes hypotactic preference in English language, namely, valuing the completeness in structure and the strictness in form.

Since English sentences convey, or control, to be more precise, meaning through overt cohesion, it seems that English is rule-governed, while Chinese is man-governed, that is, in English it represents the practical and scientific orientation for English speakers place heavy emphasis on forms rather than on "spirit" and make English language become a possible object of analysis, while Chinese is more humanistic when Chinese people lay stress on "spirit", not on forms. Therefore, English becomes a language that highlights objectivity whereas Chinese subjectivity.

## 1.2  Contrast of Parataxis in Chinese and HYpotaxis in English

From the point of view of the origin of English and Chinese characters, in English there are phonetic characters, with 26 letters of basic written symbols, and the spelling and pronunciation of words form a logical relationship according to certain pronunciation rules, while letters are only substituted symbols for meaning. The expression of language information depends on the arrangement and combination of symbols according to a certain logical relationship, so it can be said that English is a language with formal logic and a marked language or form language. Because English words are a combination of letters and phonemes and have the function of morphogenesis, English words have a wide range of morphological and functional signs and part of speech signs, which makes the English grammatical structure explicit and its form easier to grasp. In the part of speech change, in addition to expressing the change of part of speech or meaning through the derivation of words, there are also the plural forms of nouns, various tense forms of verbs, the case forms of personal pronouns and so on.

The following is a typical example of English expressing meaning in form: They loved each other and there is no love between them. (他们过去是相爱的,但现在已没有什么感情可言了。)In this example, no adverbial of time is used, but the change of verb tenses is used to show that the situation has changed over time. However, the Chinese word itself does not have this kind of morphological change, that is, it has no morphogenetic function. In addition, adding a prefix or suffix to the root to change the meaning or part of speech is also a feature of English word formation. By adding prefixes, it generally only causes the change of the meaning of words, for example, the prefixes that express the opposite meaning are "un-, in-, dis-, ab-, non-, anti-…". There are also suffixes indicating various parts of speech, such as noun suffixes, adjective suffixes, adverb suffixes and verb suffixes. This form of change of parts of speech does not exist in Chinese.

Chinese is hieroglyphics, using square characters. This kind of square character is isolated in structure, and the combination of the characters does not cause the change in form, so it is not easy to make formal analysis. Chinese uses non-phonetic word order to express meaning, which is opposed to morphological changes, so Chinese almost entirely depends on parataxis in expressing the relationship between actions and things. This makes Chinese grammar implicit, and the expression of grammatical relations directly

# Chapter Four   The Reflection of CTP in Chinese and English Languages

depends on semantics, word order and logic. Although Chinese characters lack form, the text itself is rich in meaning, with polysemy, homonym, and is flexible and convenient to use. A slight change in the order and position of words will produce new meanings, including grammatical meaning.

Look at the following examples: 故事 VS 事故 (Story VS accident), 事倍功半 VS 事半功倍 (get half the results with double the effort VS yield twice the result with half the effort), 奶牛 VS 牛奶 (cow VS milk), 老刘 VS 刘老 (a normal address of an elderly person whose family name is Liu VS a respectful address of a senior citizen whose family name is Liu), and so on. The word order has changed and the meaning has completely changed. It can be seen that the basic operating mechanism of Chinese is based on word order. Therefore, it is very easy to convey emotion and meaning with this kind of language which is not restricted by the system of morphological change.

In terms of syntactic structure, English also shows a high degree of formalization and logic. Its syntactic structure is rigorous and it takes verbs as the core, emphasizing parataxis, and closely combining meaning with syntactic form, which fully embodies the characteristics of hypotaxis. The English sentences are with subject-predicate-object structure or subject-predicate structure, which is similar to Chinese.

While generally speaking, English sentences must be complete, especially with the subject not being omitted. Some non-subject sentences in Chinese, such as "下雪了" and "出事了", when put into English, a logical subject must be added as "It's snowing" and "Something happened." This is obviously a kind of formal legality. It is common to use "it" as a subject in English. When describing natural phenomena, "it" is often used as the subject, such as "it's so hot". As in Chinese, non-subject sentences can be used like "真热", which can be described as the integration of subject and object, reflecting the concept of traditional Chinese philosophy.

In English it also has relatively strict requirements for punctuation marks, and the elements in inter-sentences should also be connected by formal, logical and relational words, coupled with rich morphological changes, which makes English a very accurate and highly formalized language. To quote Mr. Shen Xiaolong: "English sentences tend to unify the spirit with form, restrict the pattern of sentences with plump morphological changes, define sentence boundaries, and combine strictly. It is a kind of spatial tree structure which takes finite verbs as the core and controls all kinds of relations." (1988)

In English, sentences always have a certain frame, and the subject-predicate structure of the sentence is the starting point of the whole sentence. Other modifiers, restrictions, supplements and other additional components are like the side branches on the trunk, which are spatially framed with the help of various related words to form a tree structure.

In Chinese, sentences are generally short, with one short sentence after another, gradually unfolded. The content of the information goes through like a bamboo pole, and there is rarely a stacked structure, so it is often called a "bamboo pole" structure. In many cases, Chinese sentence structures are arranged in the order of subject, predicate and object, but the whole sentence is not centered on predicate verbs, but on word order or semantics, regardless of whether the sentence is complete or not.

Generally speaking, in English, the predicate verbs can not be omitted, but in Chinese, it is quite different, in which other parts of speech rather than just verbs can be used as the predicates. For example, "我（I）累（tired）了", and "今天（today）星期三（Wednesday）". In the two examples adjectives are used as the predicate in the first sentence and the nouns are used as the predicate in the second sentence. Therefore, in Chinese there are no certain subject-predicate frame restrictions, and there is no difference between predicate verbs and non-predicate verbs. It is possible that several verb structures are used together with comma splices or several nominal phrases are

# Chapter Four　The Reflection of CTP in Chinese and English Languages

arranged succinctly and vividly.

　　At the same time, unlike English, it is not necessary to use various cohesive devices such as conjunctions, as long as the meaning can be expressed. Its syntactic structure emphasizes parataxis as much as lexical structure, and the combination of various components in a sentence mainly depends on the penetration of semantics and the contrast of context, which makes Chinese sentences concise and flexible and full of metaphorical colors.

　　For example,"你来了,我走.（You come, I go.）" Conjunctions are not used in this sentence and can be understood in English as "If you come, I'll go.", or can also be understood as "When you come, I'll go.", or "Since you have come, I may go.", or "I'll go because you come." Therefore, the readers need to rely on the context to accurately understand the meaning of the sentence.

　　In addition, certain meaning can be expressed by means of the change in word order and repetition. For example,"人不犯我,我不犯人。（If a person does not attack me, I will not commit a crime.）" It can be seen that in Chinese conjunctions are not used as frequently as in English, but it depends on context, word order and other means to express meaning. All these are the embodiment of parataxis in Chinese.

　　English discourse emphasizes hypotaxis, and the connection between words or sentences mainly depends on conjunctions or linguistic morphological means. Segments are extended in a ring-like multi-faceted manner, with emphasis on cohesion. The characteristics of the "spatial tree structure" of English sentences are not only applicable to sentences, but also to the organizational structure of texts, which are larger than the units of sentences.

　　English discourse emphasizes the integrity of structure, the formal connection between sentences, strict logic and rigor. A large number of excessive marking symbols or conjunctions are often used in the discourse so as to achieve the overall semantic coherence of the text. Its textual cohesion shows explicit characteristics. Read the following paragraph as an example.

*We listened to such explanations sympathetically and explained that, first of all, we did not much care whether Benjamin succeeded in inserting the key into the slot. He was having a good time and was exploring, two activities that did matter to us. But the critical point was that, in the process, we were trying to teach Benjamin that one can solve a problem effectively by oneself. Such self-reliance is a principal value of child rearing in middle-class America. So long as the child is shown exactly how to do something —— whether it be placing a key in a key slot, drawing a hen or making up for a misdeed —— he is less likely to figure out himself how to accomplish such a task. And, more generally, he is less likely to view life —— as Americans do —— as a series of situations in which one has to learn to think for oneself, to solve problems on one's own and even to discover new problems for which creative solutions are wanted.* ——quoted from the first lesson of the New Edition of College English Book 2

Many textual functional conjunctions are used in this passage, such as "and, but, or, so long as, as", with relational words such as "that, whether, which, how", prepositions such as "in, into, by, of, for, on" and transitional markers indicating the structure of thinking, such as "first of all, more generally, ever". Without these conjunctions, relational words, prepositions and transitional markers of thinking, English sentences can not be connected and express the exact meaning. This reflects the characteristics of the hypotaxis of the English language, which is consistent with the thinking habit of the English nation, which emphasizes rationality, analysis and form.

Chinese discourse is different, which emphasizes parataxis. The structure of the text is scattered and the spirit is gathered together, and its sentence structure is loose with no specific form of restraint. The syntactic relations such as the connection between words or sentences are mainly realized by the word order, semantics or the logical relationship between sentences. Instead of

# Chapter Four   The Reflection of CTP in Chinese and English Languages

pursuing formal integrity, it only seeks to achieve meaning. Its paragraphs are scattered and extended, sparse and connected, and spread freely. The most prominent feature of Chinese discourse is to connect its different levels with a chain of meaning, with its explicit form guided by ideas. Its concept, judgment and reasoning are not strict, and its syntactic function is in the form of implicit ideas.

It can be seen that Chinese discourse is semantic-centered, and as long as it is semantically relevant, the text will flow naturally, which pays less attention to the integrity and unity of form, unlike English discourse.

In terms of content, in the same paragraph in Chinese discourse, some information is directly related to the topic, which is indispensable, while some are dispensable. Thinking is influenced by the traditional "unity of man and nature", and the way of thinking is characterized by intuition and concreteness. When an article is written, it is often manifested as diverging the mind and bringing it back to the original starting point. Chinese are used to speaking in circles and often avoid the theme, starting from the broad space and time, from the whole to the part, from the big to the small, from the far to the near, and from the general to the individual. Readers must grasp the meaning from the whole, and sometimes it is inevitable that it can only be understood but not expressed in words.

The differences in text structure between Chinese and English are mainly the differences between parataxis and hypotaxis, and also reflect the differences between the two modes of thinking: the Westerners pay attention to linear causal thinking, formal logic and deductive reasoning; Chinese focus on intuition and holistic thinking, rich in imagination and emphasis on comprehension.

It stresses parataxis in Chinese, relying on semantic connection with less grammatical connectors and on word order to organize the sentences, which neglects grammatical rules in some cases. People are expected to use synthetic and intuitional thought to interpret and comprehend the meaning. Lack of conjunctions or transitional elements in Chinese usually does not impair one's comprehension of the meaningful relationship between sentences for it has been revealed through context.

Under the influence of the Chinese thought patterns, the Chinese language tends to adopt a principle of idea outweighing linguistic form. Many of its words can be used as nouns, adjectives, or verbs, and their sequence is determined not so much by grammatical rules as by the emotional content of the sentence. In many cases, the sentence structure of Chinese is arranged in SVO order, but it does not center on the verb as an English sentence does. It evolves along the idea conveyed.

As long as the meaning is delivered, there is no need to use cohesive devices like conjunctions. Logical connection is implicit rather than clearly indicated like English in the process of sentence arrangement and idea conveying, thus producing high frequency of parataxis in Chinese and high frequency of hypotaxis in English respectively. For example, the sentence "Just <u>because</u> they make more money than I do they think they are cleverer <u>and</u> more important than I am." is not necessary to be translated as "正因为他们比我挣的钱多,他们就觉得比我聪明,比我重要。". A more natural one is "他们比我挣的钱多,就觉得比我聪明,比我重要。". In the original English sentence, words like "because" and "and" have to be used to link the clauses or identical elements to make clear the meaning. Thus, the sentence seems long but its meaning is clear at first sight. As is seen from the two versions of translation, the former one, the direct translation from English origin seems redundant and verbose, which is unnecessary for Chinese whereas the latter one seems more simple, natural and acceptable to Chinese readers.

A more typical example is Shelly's well-known motto "If winter comes, can spring be far behind?" In Chinese translation "冬天来了,春天还会远吗?" the connector "if" is omitted but the meaning can be deduced. Different from

## Chapter Four   The Reflection of CTP in Chinese and English Languages

the emphasis on formal syntax of English sentences, Chinese sentences base themselves on semantic syntax, which means, according to scholar Shen Xiaolong (1997) that the Chinese sentence composition is not designed to obtain the completeness of linguistic structure. Rather, it aims to achieve a free flow of meaning. The sentence structure is not restricted by arrangements of form, but by idea-conveying process, so as to carry rich meanings without the burden of redundancy.

As a consequence, the order of the clauses in Chinese sentences is in line with the flow of thoughts. The meaning of a sentence changes as the order of the clauses varies. Such a pattern of thought-oriented clause arrangement is called the "flowing-water style".

For instance, in "屡战屡败,屡败屡战" and "屡败屡战,屡战屡败", the change of order produces two different meanings as the former means "suffer one defeat after another, but never give up the fight" and the latter means "go on fighting after each defeat, only to suffer yet another defeat".

For the paratactic tradition in Chinese language, the grammatical relations of the language are usually to be sensed rather than explained by readers or listeners. It is especially true when it comes to the relations of actions and objects. This feature is also clearly shown in ancient Chinese. In *Master Sun's Art of War*, it is estimated that 92.6% of the sentences are constructed paractically, that is, without connectives, with only 7.4% organized hypotactically. Here is a famous quotation from the book.

知己知彼,百战不殆;不知彼而知己,一胜一负;不知彼不知己,每战必殆。(《孙子·谋攻》)

All these clauses demonstrate the paratactic character of Chinese, that is, one clause follows the other without connectives showing the relationship between them. But, when it is translated into English, the Chinese conjunctions must be added first to make it clear the relations between clauses.

（若）知己（又）知彼，（则）（虽）百战（而）不殆；（若）不知彼而知己，（则）（将）一胜一负；（若）不知彼（又）不知己，（则）每战（将）必殆。

Hence, in English, more connectives are required, as is seen from the following version of translation (Liu Miqing, 1991:159).

You can fight a hundred battles without defeat *if* you know the enemy *as well as* yourself. You will win one battle and lose one battle *if* you know yourself but are in the dark about the enemy. You will lose every battle *if* you are in the dark about both the enemy and yourself.

English CTP are characterized as logical and analytic, placing a great significance on the formal logic and systematic experiments and understanding the world by means of geometry and logic. It causes English language to prefer hypotaxis, that is, the language stresses analysis and logic, mainly applying syntactic devices and lexical equivalence to organize the sentences, which stresses the variation in tense and word form. The sentence frame is concentrated on one key finite verb and exemplifies a conjunctive nexus with the help of all kinds of cohesive ties acting within. The connection in English is explicit and various. Compared with the loose structure in Chinese, English sentences, with the principle of concord and overt formal cohesive elements, are well organized to such an extent that they lack flexibility.

Specifically, the grammatical connectors including conjunctions such as "and" "as" "if" and "because"; prepositions such as "in" "on" and "of"; adverbs like "afterwards" "consequently" and "moreover"; relative pronouns like "who" "that" and "when"; functional phrases, etc. are utilized to show the logical relations between components within a sentence or relations between sentences or paragraphs. Only with overt cohesion can an English

# Chapter Four   The Reflection of CTP in Chinese and English Languages

speaker ascertain the meaning of the whole sentence. Here are some examples of Chinese sentences, whose translations reflect this characteristic.

人不犯我,我不犯人。
We will not attack unless we are attacked.

问遍千家成行家。
Learn from numerous advisers, and you'll become a master.

聪明一世,糊涂一时。
Smart as a rule, but this time a fool.

种瓜得瓜,种豆得豆。
As you sow, so will you reap.

It is clear from these examples that English prefer hypotaxis, depending mainly on certain connective words to link the elements whereas Chinese prefer parataxis, adopting the ways of word order, punctuation, or other means to combine the clauses. Therefore, the surface meanings of English sentences are fairly explicit and the structures are strict and complicated often with rather long sentences. The structures of English and Chinese sentences are vividly described by a Chinese professor Wang Yin (1990) that an English sentence is like a tree with a trunk and some branches attached to it, the trunk being the main clause and the branches being the subordinate clauses and dependent phrases when a Chinese sentence is like a clump of bamboo, each shoot of which grows independently. This simile properly generalizes the characteristics of hypotaxis in English and parataxis in Chinese. Take the following sentence as an example.

*The little girl, who was crying as if her heart would break, said, when*

*I spoke to her*, *that she was very hungry*, *because she had had no food for two days*.

  This is a typical sentence in English that embodies its hypotaxis. Its mainclause of the sentence is "The little girl... said...", which is followed by five subordinate clauses, including the attributive clause "who...", the adverbial clause "as if...", the adverbial clause of time "when...", the adverbial clause of cause "because..." and the object clause "that..." attached to it like a tree with a trunk, the main clause and some branches, the subordinate clauses hung on it. The five subordinate clauses are connected to the main clause by guide words or conjunctions such as "who" "as if" "when" "that" and "because". These clauses are spread around the main clause one by one, like branches of a tree or a grapevine. The connective words "who..." "as if..." "when..." "that..." and "because..." seem like the hooks hanging the five clauses to the main. Therefore, some linguists call it a "grape" structure. Its characteristic is that sentences often take a subject-predicate structure as the backbone, layer by layer, and expand outward. The sentences are quite long and there are many clauses with one inside another.

  When put into Chinese, the whole structure has to be changed.

  那个小女孩哭得似乎心都碎了,当我问她时,她说已有两天没吃东西,实在是饿极了。

  In this translation, four short Chinese clauses, arranged in terms of time sequence and cause-effect order, are like some clumps of bamboo, stated one after another. "那个小女孩哭得似乎心都碎了" leads to the result "我问她"; because "我问她", "她说已有两天没吃东西"; "她说已有两天没吃东西" is the reason for "实在是饿极了".

  The frequent application of grammatical connectors in English and the little use of them in Chinese cause the complexity in English sentence

## Chapter Four   The Reflection of CTP in Chinese and English Languages

structure and the simplicity in Chinese sentence structure. English sentences are relatively longer and more complicated than Chinese sentences because in English various connectors and devices can be used to combine sentences. It can be seen from the different composition in sentence type in the two languages.

According to sentence structure, sentences can be divided into simple, compound, complex and compound-complex ones in English and simple and complex ones in Chinese. To some extent the last three types of sentences in English are similar to the complex ones in Chinese considering the logical relations. In English a compound sentence refers to a sentence composed of either two or more elements that are independent sentences and are combined by means of mainly co-coordinative conjunctions as in these examples.

(1) They must stay in water, or they will die.
(2) This is me and these are my friends.
(3) The Government introduces a program of laws, the Opposition criticizes it, and the Queen as the supreme head of the State gives it her final authority.

Here "or" and "and" as coordinative conjunctions are necessary but "and" in the second and third sentences can not be translated into its equivalent "和" as it is not necessary in Chinese.

A complex sentence refers to a sentence composed of a principal clause and at least one subordinate clause connected by subordinate conjunctions, interrogative pronouns, interrogative adverbs, relative pronouns, relative adverbs, etc. as in these examples.

(1) *Workers can report their problems and suggestions to their representatives, who will then convey them to the plant management.*

(2) *Please tell your father that I'm very grateful to him for the warm welcome I have received here and that when I go back, I will tell my family all about my visit here.*

(3) *One factor contributing to the rise in marriage expenses is the belief that a couple will lose "face" if they don't keep up with the Jones.*

(4) *Where he has surpassed every other English writer is in his ballads and songs.*

(5) *Metals expand when heated and contract when cooled.*

A compound-complex sentence is a sentence contained two or more independent complex clauses joined by co-coordinative conjunctions as in the example.

*People go further and further away to reach open air and countryside——which continuously recedes from them, and just as their working weeks decline and they begin to have more time for leisure, they find they cannot get to the open spaces or the recreation or the beaches which they now have the time to enjoy.*

Here the two complex clauses including an attributive clause led by "which" and an adverbial clause led by "just as" are combined by conjunction "and" to make a compound-complex sentence. Though there are times when the elements may be combined with punctuations like comma, semicolon, colon, etc. in compound sentences, this circumstance doesn't so often occur in English. Consequently, the English sentences are rather complicated compared with the Chinese ones.

In Chinese a complex sentence may be connected either by some connectors or, more frequently, by punctuations like comma, semicolon, colon, etc., which seems simple and concise in structure. In Chinese it tends

# Chapter Four    The Reflection of CTP in Chinese and English Languages

to leave out many linking elements and relies heavily on the context for the complete meaning of a message. It is believed that the connections and linkages between clauses can be inferred rather than all are explicitly seen from the words used, and the recognition of the relationship between Chinese clauses depends more on personal perception and judgment. For the Chinese, semantic coherence should be of primary concern, while grammatical relations are only regarded as secondary. Here are some typical examples of Chinese complex sentences.

这种作风,拿了律己,则害了自己;拿了教人,则害了别人;拿了指导革命,则害了革命。(毛泽东《改造我们的学习》)

所谓回忆者,虽说可以使人欢欣,有时也不免使人寂寞,使精神的丝缕还牵着已逝的寂寞的时光,又有什么意味呢,而我偏苦于不能全忘却,这不能全忘的一部分,到现在更成了《呐喊》的来由。(鲁迅《呐喊》自序)

Although long English sentences are sometimes difficult to understand, they are yet absolutely grammatical, that is, they possess the property of strictness in grammar. The following example is a representative, which is quite difficult for Chinese to comprehend but rigid in grammar.

*Oh, Simplicio, if I should succeed in convincing you of the artfulness — though it is no great artistry — of this author, I should rouse you to wonder — and also to indignation — when you discovered how he, covering his cunning with the veil of your naiveté and that of other mere philosophers, tries to insinuate himself into your good graces by gratifying your ear, and puffing up your ambition, pretending to have convinced and silenced these trifling astronomers who wanted to assail the ineradicable inalterability of the Peripatetic heavens, and what is more, to have struck them dumb and overpowered them with their own weapons.*

This is a complex sentence composed of 104 words, which seems, to Chinese, quite difficult to comprehend for its complicated structure, while the structure of this sentence can be clearly analyzed with the help of the connectors. The principal clause is "I should succeed you to wonder — and also to indignation — ". All the other parts in this sentence are subordinate clauses, which cannot exist independently. The clause before the principal one, "if I should...of this author", is an adverbial clause of condition and the clause after the principal one, "when you... their own weapons", is an adverbial clause of time, which embodies an adjective clause "who wanted to... the Peripatetic heavens". Though for Chinese such a sentence is obscure and hard to interpret, it is grammatically regular and strictly conforms to the rules in the eyes of natives.

Comparatively, Chinese sentences are concise yet loose with short clauses and the extra long ones seem uncustomary. The punctuations, especial commas, are frequently exerted to connect the elements, which may seem to be grammatically vague and inexact to some extent. Generally, the meanings of Chinese sentences are implicit and the structures are simple with quite short sentences. It is the reflection of Chinese intuitional thought. The following is the translation of the former example by Zhou Xuliang, whose sentences in this translation are considered natural, acceptable and even ideal to Chinese readers.

啊,辛普利邱,但愿我能够说服你,使你看出这位作者的伎俩——虽则并不是怎样高明的伎俩。他利用你的天真和其他不懂天文学的哲学家的天真,为自己打掩护,企图博取你们的欢心。他把那些想要攻击逍遥学派天界的稳固性和不可动摇性的文学家,说成是毫不足道的,并自命已经驳倒他们,使他们无辞以答;不但如此,他还自命用他们自己的武器驳得他们哑口无言,无力还击。他就

# Chapter Four　The Reflection of CTP in Chinese and English Languages

是用这种伎俩使你觉得娓娓动听,并鼓起你的无名勇气,如果你一旦发现他是怎样做到这样的,我当会引起你的惶惑——并且使你感到愤慨。(Zhou Xuliang, edited by Zhang Guangming,1999:244)

In this translation, the original sentence is divided into five sentences with simple structures in each one. The elements in the sentences are linked with punctuations and some connectors.

It is recognized that Chinese belongs to paratactic language, which utilizes semantic connection rather than syntactic devices, depending on the variation in word order, the context and the implication to make clear the meaning of the speakers. Therefore, the order of Chinese sentences generally conforms to the natural sequence of logic and time, whereas in English sometimes the natural sequence is broken to realize the hypotaxis in structure. Take the position of modifiers both in English and Chinese as an example. In English the modifiers can be put either before or after the headwords, which are the so-called "premodefiers" and "postmodifiers". When the modifiers are quite complex, postmodifiers are usually used. Unlike what is in English, only premodifiers are applied in Chinese as is shown in the following table.

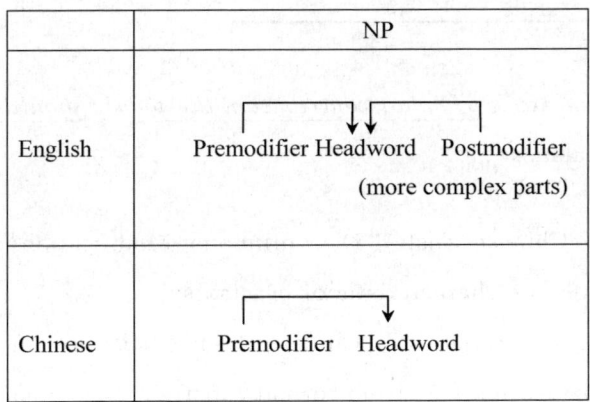

While in Chinese the modifiers are usually close to and usually before their headwords, seldom separated and inserted by other components. For

• 73 •

example:

She has the ability to swim like a fish. 她有像鱼一样游泳的本领。

Another aspect in which the hypotaxis is reflected in English is that in some structures the headwords and their modifiers are separated either customarily or to arrive at certain aims. "It is not uncommon for the noun phrase to be interrupted by other items of clause structure." (Quirk, 1973) This phenomenon is called "Discontinuous Modification". Here are some examples:

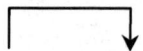

a *nice* cup of *tea* (customary expression)

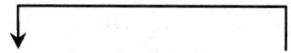

You'll meet *a man* tomorrow *carrying a heavy parcel*. (avoiding ambiguity)

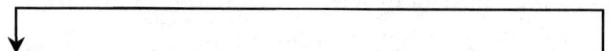

*The box* was by the door, which *had contained the papers and other valuables*. (keeping the structural balance)

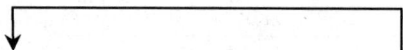

*The problem* arose *of what contribution the public should pay*. (keeping the structural balance)

Usually in Chinese such "Discontinuous Modification" is impossible because it violates the characteristic of parataxis.

As for the characteristics of Chinese thinking, it pays more attention to semantic integrity, often free from formal constraints, as long as it can reach the meaning. Cohesive devices are not necessarily used in sentences, and a coherent text can be formed through the internal meaning of the relationship

## Chapter Four   The Reflection of CTP in Chinese and English Languages

between sentences. Although there are some conjunctions in Chinese, they are seldom used or often omitted in writing, so their numbers and the frequency of use are much fewer and lower than those in English. Take the following sentence as an example.

"As a matter of fact, there is no road on the ground, but when there are more people walking, it becomes a road." (Lu Xun's "hometown") The sentence omits the words like "because" and "so…"

"Whenever his wife urges him to try to redeem his leather robe, he smiles and says, 'my heart is hot, but my body is not cold!'" The writer Lau Show omitted the expression "as long as / if" in the sentence from "Four Generations Living Together".

The characteristics of English thinking review that English is a formal language, in which the writing is more rigorous, so in the English discourse it pays more attention to the form, and emphasizes the integrity of the sentence structure. Therefore, there are many conjunctive words in English, and the frequency of use is also quite high. Various conjunctions commonly used between sentences are prepositions, conjunction adverbs, conjunction pronouns, relation adverbs, relation pronouns and so on, which are collectively referred to as conjunctions. There are too many conjunctions in English, which can be divided into more than 20 kinds according to their meanings and the logical meanings needed to connect the article. The most commonly used examples are as follows.

　　a. for opening: to begin with, in the first place, in general, generally speaking…

　　b. for summary: to sum up, to conclude, finally, in other words, on the whole, hence, in short…

　　c. giving examples: for example, a case in point, such as for one thing…, as an illustration…

　　d. for causes: because, now that, being that, owing to, due to, for the reason that, in view of...

e. representing the result: as a result, consequently, accordingly, therefore, under these conditions...

f. for comparison (similarity): likewise, in common, in the same way, in comparison with...

g. for contrast (differences): rather, neither... nor, conversely, as opposed to, in contrast...

h. for reiterating: in other words, that is to say, as I have said, again, once again...

i. for emphasis: particularly, certainly, surely, of course, indeed, in particular, believe it or not...

j. for concession: even though, although, in spite of, however, but, yet...

k. for transition: but, even so, though, reckless of, despite that, in spite of that, regardless of...

l. for juxtaposition: and, also, too, as well as, either...or..., both and...

m. for progressing: furthermore, moreover, not only... but also..., moreover, even...

n. for conditional relations: if, unless, lest, provided that, if so, if it is the case, in this sense, once...

o. for aims: for this purpose, in this way, since, on that account, in case, with a view to...

The difference between holistic thinking and analytical thinking is also reflected in the language. In Chinese it places more emphasis on the integrity of content, while in English it emphasizes the rigor of structural form. This difference is mainly reflected in English and Chinese sentences. Chinese sentences emphasize the integrity of meaning and the shape of meaning, so syntactic structure and semantic information are often implicit.

For example, some words responsible for semantic connection are often omitted in Chinese sentences, as long as the meaning of the sentence is complete. The logical relationship can be realized through the ordering of words, pauses and intuitive epiphany, and the sentence components can be incomplete. The phenomenon of omitting the subject can be seen everywhere.

Besides, English sentences pay attention to the rigor of structure, and their syntactic structure and the transmission of the information are explicit with the help of naked and plump morphological changes. English sentences often express semantic relations and the relationship between sentences with the help of a large number of conjunctions and phrases, and the principle of sentence construction is that both subject and predicate are indispensable.

Look at the following Chinese sentences and their corresponding translations.

不到黄河心不死。
Until all is over, ambition never dies.

欲盖弥彰。
The more one tries to hide, the more one is exposed.

In the above examples, Chinese sentences seldom use obvious semantic conjunctions, and the meaning of the sentence is often understood through word order, parallelism, comparison and so on. It can be seen from the corresponding translation that English sentences pay attention to connection means and forms, and achieve sentence integrity with the help of morphological changes of relational words, conjunctions, prepositions, and words, which can be seen in the boldface part of the above examples.

The different characteristics of Chinese and English can be reflected from the mode of thinking of the people who use the languages.

English is a morphological language with the characteristics showing that whether it is choosing words to make sentences or organizing texts, it is bound to pay attention to the connection and form of language, that is, hypotaxis.

English hypotaxis specifically refers to the strong logical relationship between English language symbols, which is dominated by logical form, closely organized sentences, connected layer by layer, paying attention to morphological changes and the use of logical and grammatical conjunctions, including conjunctions, prepositions, adverbs, relation words and various phrases that act as a connecting link between the preceding and the following, to illustrate the logical relations within sentences, between sentences, and even between paragraphs.

Chinese sentencs are mainly connected by the meaning of words, and its expression is guided by ideas, that is, it mainly depends on the change of word order, context and illocutionary factual logic to achieve the purpose of clear thinking. The sentence looks loose, and each clause depends on the penetration of internal logical relations. The structure of authentic Chinese sentences, sentence groups and texts is an open structure with no close aggregation, and what connects them is logic and meaning. As Mr. Wang Li said, "the British tend to break up into pieces when they write articles, while the Chinese tend to break up into parts."

The characteristics of overlapping in English sentence and discourse components require that careful analysis must be made about the multiple components of sentences and sentence groups and their structural relations with each other. At the same time, it also shows that English grammar is a form-oriented grammar, which also reflects the cognitive characteristics of rational, individual and complete form in the thinking mode of Britain, the United States and other Western nations.

Relatively speaking, Chinese sentences and texts mainly rely on word order, context and logical relations to organize and form. The sentences are loose and scattered, with the overall context of the passage to be grasped

# Chapter Four  The Reflection of CTP in Chinese and English Languages

through the comprehension of its connotation and implied meaning, which reflects the mode of thinking that the Chinese nation attaches importance to the grasp and understanding of the whole, in other words, the synthesis.

It can be said that different languages reflect different world views and different modes of thinking. Learning one language is tantamount to entering another circle or another world. Therefore, it can be said that learning a foreign language is not only just to grasp a tool, or a skill, but also to experience a process of changing thinking patterns or habits. It should also be pointed out that with the exchange and integration of Eastern and Western cultures, languages also have a corresponding influence and infiltration, each showing some important characteristics of each other. There are definitely certain forms of hypotaxis in Chinese and some forms of parataxis in English. It can not absolutely and simply mention hypotaxis in English and parataxis in Chinese.

The hypotaxis in English and parataxis in Chinese are the significant distinctive characteristics of the composition of the two languages, which is an important subject in the comparative study of Chinese and English. It has close relationships with the cultures and thought patterns between English and Chinese nations. The English nation stresses the reason and analysis and the Chinese nation emphasizes the intuition and synthesis, which are reflected in the two languages. Since English is hypotactic and Chinese is paratactic, English language requires formal logic and restricted grammar, while Chinese language requires more comprehension and insight.

## 2. Topic-comment Structure VS Subject-predicate Structure

### 2.1  Causes of Topic-comment Structure in Chinese and Subject-predicate Structure in English

Since English stresses analytical and logical thinking while Chinese values synthetic and intuitional thinking, it certainly causes the strictness in English and the looseness in Chinese structure. Probably the most typical kind of sentence in English is the declarative sentence made up of a subject, verb, and direct object and associated with the conceptual focus of an actor, action, and the object of an action. For example, the answer to the question "What happened?" could be either

| Mike | dropped | the ball |
| --- | --- | --- |
| Subject | verb | Direct Object |
| Actor | Action | Object of Action |

or

| The bus | hit | the pole |
| --- | --- | --- |
| Subject | verb | Direct Object |
| Actor | Action | Object of Action. |

This sentence form is so common in English that speakers of English use the form metaphorically without being the least bit conscious of imposing the form "actor, action, object of action" where it does not literally apply. As a result, in English it commonly produces such sentences named subject-predicate sentences.

In Chinese, however, it does not ordinarily use this kind of sentence structure. If one asked a speaker of Chinese the equivalent of the question "What happened?" he would probably give the answer in the form of topic and comment. In other words, where the American would say, "Mike dropped the ball.", the Chinese would say, "球掉下来了。". The structure is shown like this:

| 球 | 掉下来了 |
| --- | --- |
| topic | comment |

# Chapter Four  The Reflection of CTP in Chinese and English Languages

It is not necessary for the Chinese to indicate the actor or the time of the action. Speakers of English, in contrast, specify the actor and whether the action was in the past or not. However, they do have a sentence form where the actor is not specified—subject and passive verb: "The ball was dropped." Many speakers of English feel uneasy about this construction, which does not appear complete. Since only two of the three habitual components are present, they feel compelled to ask, "Dropped by whom?" In general, English and Chinese have different basic sentence structures that focus on different aspects of a situation.

In English there are five basic sentence structures: SV, SVC, SVO, $SVO_1O_2$ and SVOC, each of which contains subject and predicate verb. English draws a distinction between subject and predicate influenced by dichotomous and objective thought patterns. It has become an invariable custom to have a subject before the predicate, and a sentence that does not contain a subject is felt to be incomplete. So, if there is a predicate but no subject in a sentence, then a subject is assumed. The word "it" often suffices for the missing subject, as in the sentence: "It is 6 o'clock." On the contrary, the omission of the subjects is very common in Chinese. A Chinese sentence may have no definite subject but it does have a topic at the beginning, which, together with the other components, constitutes "topic-comment" sentence structure. But the topics don't necessarily serve as the subjects. For example:

(1) 单位的事， 你　　不用管。
　　　　　　　(subject)
　　topic　　　comment

(2) 爱护环境　 人人　有份。
　　　　　　 (subject)
　　topic　　 comment

(3) 这几年里　　体育事业　蓬勃发展。
　　　　　　　（subject）
　　topic　　　　　　　comment

(4) 剧院里　正在演出。（subjectless sentence）
　　topic　　comment

(5) 去年　　开发了一款新的游戏。（subjectless sentence）
　　topic　　　　comment

In examples (1)(2) and (3) the topics and the subjects are not identical as the topics in these three sentences actually function as the object（单位的事）, the complement（爱护环境）and the adverbial modifier（这几年里）respectively. Both the examples (4) and (5) belong to subjectless sentences with the topics functioning as the adverbial modifiers. Neither of those two structures in the above examples occurs in English.

### 2.2 Contrast of Topic-Comment Structure and Subject-predicate Structure

The theory of subject-prominent and topic-prominent languages is established in Li and Thompson's paper "Subject and Topic: A New Typology of Language"（1976）. In this paper they hold that "many structural phenomena of a language can be explained on the basis of whether the basic structure of its sentences is analyzed as subject-predicate or topic-comment". Here they argue that it is more meaningful to divide languages typologically not in terms of the traditional distinction of SVO, SOV, etc., word order but rather on the basis of whether languages manifest as basic grammatical relations of subject-predicate or topic-comment, and subsequently they conclude a typological distinction of languages for the following four categories:

# Chapter Four  The Reflection of CTP in Chinese and English Languages

(1) languages that are subject-prominent (e.g., Indo-European, including English, French, etc);

(2) languages that are topic-prominent (e.g., Chinese);

(3) languages that are both subject-prominent and topic-prominent (e.g., Japanese);

(4) languages that are neither subject-prominent nor topic-prominent (e.g., Tagalog, Illocano).

Li and Thompson further explained that in "subject-prominent (Sp) languages, the structure of sentences favors a description in which the grammatical relation *subject-predicate* plays a major role; in topic-prominent (Tp) languages, the basic structure of sentences favors a description in which the grammatical relation *topic-comment* plays a major role." (Charles N. Li & Sandra A. Thompson, 1976) They pointed out that "this is not to say that in Tp languages, one cannot identify subjects, or that Sp languages do not have topics". In fact, all the languages they have investigated have the topic-comment construction, and although not all languages have the subject-predicate construction, there appear to be ways of identifying subjects in most Tp languages. Just as they stated that "it seems clear that subject and topic are not unrelated notions. Subjects are essentially grammaticalized topics; in the process of being integrated into the case frame of the verb (at which point we call them subjects), topics become somewhat impure, and certain of their topic properties are weakened, but their topic-ness is still recognizable" (1976). Therefore, it can be deduced that in Chinese it can still have subject in a sentence and in English it can still have topics in a sentence though the former falls into a topic-prominent language and the latter a subject-prominent one.

Based on the theory above, it is clear that English as a kind of subject-prominent language makes the sentences meaningful with reference to the grammatical relation of subject-predicate. Comparatively, Chinese as a typical topic-prominent language may produce topics and comments that share a weak syntactic linkage when the topics impart "old" "given" or "shared" information and the remainder of the sentences comment on that acknowledged information with new information.

In addition, as in Chinese it is the topic rather than the subject that is always coded and occurs in the initial position of a sentence, it allows null subject, that is, the omission of subject in Chinese, which is not accepted in English. In Chinese the subjects that are known to both the author and the readers in the context can be omitted, thus the so-called "subjectless sentences", which are a typical example of reflection of Chinese synthetic, unitive, intuitive, and subjective consciousness. As a result of starting from the viewpoint of the speaker, Chinese sentences often witness the absence of grammatical subjects.

It is estimated that one third of sentences in Chinese have no subjects. Such an absence poses no difficulty to the Chinese people as they tacitly agree that the subjects should be animate things. Whether the subject is dispensable or not depends on whether the listener can understand what is said. For example, in "再开几分钟就到目的地了", the grammatical subject "你" is omitted as the Chinese would have no difficulty in understanding "who" will take the action in the sentence. But when translated into English, the subject vacancy must be filled and the rendition should be "If you drive for a few more minutes, you will get to the destination," or "A few more minutes will take you to your destination." The following are some more examples in Chinese whose subjects are omitted. Those subjects must be added when put into English.

只见她一身珠光宝气,优雅宜人。

# Chapter Four  The Reflection of CTP in Chinese and English Languages

She showed up in a graceful manner, gleaming with jewelry.

任凭风浪起,稳坐钓鱼船。
You can sit tight in the fishing boat despite the rising wind and waves.

袭人道:"一百年还记得呢!比不得你,拿着我的话当耳边风,夜里说了,早起就忘了。"
"I'll remember if I live to be a hundred!" said Aroma. "I'm not like you, letting what I say go in at one ear and out at the other forgetting what's said at night by the next morning."

看一眼路旁的绿叶,再看一眼海,真的,这才明白了什么叫作"春深似海"。
I cast a look first at the green leaves along the road and then at the sea. To tell the truth, only then did I fully understand the real meaning of "spring being as deep as the sea".

要想进入一扇门,就必须让自己的头比门框更低;要想登上成功的顶峰,就必须低头弯腰做好攀登的准备。
If you want to pass a door, you must bow your head so that it is lower than the doorframe. If you want to climb to the top of success, you must bow your head and bend your body to get ready for the climbing.

不入虎穴,焉得虎子。
How can you get the tiger cubs if you don't enter the tiger's lair?
Nothing venture, nothing gain.

In the following examples, the subjects marked in boldface are all in general rather than in particular. On the contrary, when English sentences are put into Chinese, impersonal subjects should be replaced by personal subjects in order to conform to the expressing habits of the Chinese people.

Not a sound reached their ears.(他们没听到任何声音。)

Something inside me seemed to stop momentarily.(我顿时呆住了。)

The sight of the old picture reminds me of my childhood.(看到那张老照片，我想起了自己的童年。)

In addition, because Westerners respect the philosophy of the dichotomy of God and the dichotomy of subject and object, they advocate the distinction between subject and object. In English, there is a clear distinction between being active and being passive, and the passive voice is widely used, especially in the styles of scientific, technological and political discourses, which emphasize facts, where the passive voice is used more frequently. For example, the formal subjects are commonly used with the passive voice: "It is well known that" "It is generally considered that…" "It suddenly came to me that…" "It suddenly occurred to me that…" etc.

It can be seen that in Chinese, people or living things are habitually used as subjects, and the active voice is often used, while in English, objective things or inanimate things are often used as subjects and the passive voice is often used. These language phenomena can be rooted in cultural traditions and modes of thinking.

## 3. Dynamic VS Static Preference

### 3.1 Causes of Chinese Dynamic Preference and English Static Preference

The synthesis, unity, imagination and concreteness undoubtedly cause the dynamic preference in Chinese language. Synthesis emphasizes relation and connection, trying to keep the balance from the movement. In traditional Chinese culture the universe was considered as a unity with perpetual transformation, a constant process of unceasing production and reproduction. This perspective recognizes that everything in this world is fluid, ever changing, and impermanent.

# Chapter Four  The Reflection of CTP in Chinese and English Languages

In Hinduism, all static forms are called "maya", which means existing only as illusory concepts. This idea of the impermanence of all forms is the starting point of Buddhism. Buddhism teaches that all compounded things are impermanent, and that all suffering in the world arises from our trying to cling to fixed forms——objects, people, or ideas——instead of accepting the world as it moves. Some Buddhists believe life itself continues in endless cycles in which a soul can assume an infinite variation of form. This notion of impermanence of all forms and the appreciation of the aliveness of the universe in the Eastern worldview will certainly cause the dynamic state. In addition, the concrete thought also contributes to the dynamic characteristic in Chinese language.

On the contrary, the analysis, dichotomy and abstract thoughts lead to the static state in English. Plato first put forward the idea of dichotomy of subject and object, which requires observing and analyzing the objective world from the point of view of isolation, one-sidedness and being static. In analytical and dichotomous thoughts, the subject and the object, the human beings and the nature, spirit and body, etc. are definitely divided.

Besides, the whole world is split into parts and the complex phenomena and matters are dissolved into detailed and simple elements. Therefore, the concrete parts and details are split, extracted, and isolated. Due to this perceptive process, analysis must possess the feature of being static and isolated. Furthermore, converting from the dynamic state to the static state is one of the characteristics of abstract thought.

## 3.2  Contrast of Dynamic Preference and Static Preference

Those contrastive thought patterns reflected in languages are dynamic preference in Chinese and the static one in English. Take the following Chinese sentences with their corresponding translations in English as examples.

由于他离开此地，从 1946 年 1 月开始的长期谈判和讨论乃告结束。（动）

His departure brought to an end the long period of negotiations and discussions begun in January 1946. (n.)

但是,仔细研读他们的小说后,人们不禁得出这样的结论:他们一些方面有着惊人相似。(动)
But a close study of their short stories will lead to a conclusion that they have a striking resemblance in several aspects. (n.)

司机违反任何交通规则都要被警察惩罚。(动)
Violation of any traffic rules by the drivers will be fined by the police. (n.)

我既不抽烟,也不喝酒。(动)
I'm a nonsmoker and teetotaler. (n.)

那男孩可真会捣乱。(动)
That boy is a master complicator. (n.)

Compare the emphasized words in each pair and it is easy to find out that in Chinese large numbers of dynamic verbs are used while in English a wide range of nouns are preferred, which reflects the dynamic preference in Chinese and static preference in English. Adjectives, prepositions, gerunds, etc. are also frequently applied to convert from the dynamic state to the static state besides using large numbers of abstract nouns, as in the following examples.

This very formulation is indicative of the underlying attitude. (adj.)
这一说法本身已表明其根本态度。(动)

The book is beyond me. (prep.)

# Chapter Four　The Reflection of CTP in Chinese and English Languages

这本书太难,我看不懂。(动)

They kept going forward courageously in spite of all dangers and difficulties. (pp.)
他们不顾一切艰难险阻,勇往直前。(动)

Another typical example is a paragraph from William Thackeray's *Vanity Fair* (1848).

As the Manager of the Performance <u>sits</u> before the curtain on the boards, and <u>looks</u> into the Fair, a feeling of profound melancholy <u>comes</u> over him in his <u>survey</u> of the bustling place. There is a great quantity of <u>eating</u> and <u>drinking</u>, <u>making</u> love and <u>jilting</u>, <u>laughing</u> and the contrary, <u>smoking</u>, <u>cheating</u>, <u>fighting</u>, <u>dancing</u>, and <u>fiddling</u>: there are bullies <u>pushing</u> about, bucks <u>ogling</u> the women, knaves <u>picking</u> pockets, policemen <u>on the look-out</u>, quacks (other quacks, plague take them!) <u>bawling</u> in front of their booths, and yokels <u>looking up</u> at the <u>tinseled</u> dancers and old <u>rouged</u> tumblers, while the light-fingered folk <u>are operating</u> upon their pockets behind. Yes, this is Vanity Fair; not a moral place certainly; nor a merry one, though very noisy.

In this extract all the words or phrases underlined have the inclination of movement, while only four words "sit" "look" "come" and "operate" function as the predicate verbs. The other movements are frequently expressed by gerunds like "eating" "drinking" "making" "jilting" etc, a prepositional phrase "on the look-out" and two past participles "tinseled" and "rouged". It is obvious that the static descriptions by using gerunds, prepositional phrases and participles instead of predicate verbs are preferred in English, which is quite different from Chinese. Here's one version of translation by famous Chinese translator Yang Bi (1957), whose works are widely accepted as they not only keep the spirit of the original but also conform to the Chinese practice. Now let's have a look at it.

领班的坐在戏台上幔子前面,对着底下闹哄哄的市场,瞧了半晌,心里不觉悲惨起来。市场上的人有的在吃喝,有的在调情,有的得了新宠就丢了旧爱;有在笑的,也有在哭的,还有在抽烟的,打架的,跳舞的,拉琴的,诓骗哄人的。有些是到处横行的强梁汉子;有些是对女人飞眼儿的花花公子,也有扒手和到处巡逻的警察,还有走江湖吃四方的,在自己摊子前面扯起嗓子嚷嚷(这些人偏和我同行,真该死!)跳舞的穿着浑身发亮的衣服,可怜的翻筋斗老头儿涂着两腮帮子胭脂,引得那些乡下佬睁着眼瞧,不提防后面就有三只手的家伙在掏他们的口袋。是了,这就是我们的名利场。这里虽然是个热闹去处,却是道德沦亡,说不上有什么快乐。

In this version large quantities of dynamic verbs (nearly 30 ones) are used to bring the effect of liveliness and a sense of mobility, which is to be in accordance with Chinese customs.

From this extract and its translation, it is valid to conclude that on the one hand, the frequent use of nouns, adjectives, adverbs, prepositions, gerunds, participles, and infinitives replaces the application of dynamic verbs in English, which will certainly cause the complex and compound sentences that are quite long. On the other hand, large numbers of dynamic predicate verbs are used in Chinese, which makes the structure of the Chinese sentences simple, loose, and, at the same time, full of sense of movement.

### 4. Preference in Applying Animate Subjects VS Inanimate Subjects

#### 4.1　Causes of Different Preferences in Applying Subjects

The subjects that are served by living things or the so-called animate things are animate subjects. The subjects that are served by nonliving things or the so-called inanimate things are inanimate subjects. The contrast between

# Chapter Four   The Reflection of CTP in Chinese and English Languages

subjective (personal) consciousness and objective consciousness in China and the West definitely influence the choice of subjects of sentences in Chinese and English languages.

Just as what is discussed previously, Chinese language mixes the subject and the object, and puts emphasis on the subject. With this strong personal consciousness in the Chinese mind, animate things are widely used as the point of departure for the message in Chinese sentences. That is to say, in Chinese people prefer using animate things as the subjects of the sentences, namely the animate subjects.

Furthermore, in Chinese usually only the human beings or living things could be the agents, that is, the subjects that could perform actions actively. In contrast, people in the West strictly dichotomize the subject——the perceiver of the world and the object——the world and it seems they stress more of the latter, holding an objective attitude towards the world and observing, analyzing and describing it objectively and sober-mindedly.

This thought pattern is also obviously reflected in choosing the subjects of the sentences in English. On the one hand, either the living things (animate) or the non-living things (inanimate) are functioned as the subjects according to the requirement. On the other hand, in most cases, non-livings, namely, inanimate things are often preferably employed as the grammatical subjects on account of the Westerners' logic analysis.

**4.2   Contrast of Chinese Animate Subjects and English Inanimate Subjects**

Just as G. Leech and J. Svartvik (1994) pointed out that "Formal written language often goes with an impersonal style; i.e., the one in which the speaker does not refer directly himself or his readers, but avoids the pronouns I, you, we." For instance, when a Chinese man saw a bird fly over, he would say "我看见了一只小鸟。", but for a native English speaker, the same meaning would be quite likely rendered as "A bird came into my view." rather than "I saw a bird." Such examples are very common in English. When put into Chinese an animate subject has to be applied to meet the requirement in Chinese. See the following examples.

His triumph was complete.
他取得了完全的胜利。

In recent years, local newspapers have been sprinkled with passionate letters advising various suggestions on the construction of the city.
近年来,热情的读者纷纷致函各地方报纸,对城市建设提出了种种建议。

It has long been maintained that it was only during his Harvard graduate years that Eliot developed his interest in primitive cultures.
人们长期以来坚持认为,艾略特对原始文化的兴趣是他在哈佛读研究生的岁月里培养起来的。

In these examples subjects are changed from the inanimate ones to the animate ones when English sentences are put into the corresponding Chinese. Although in the first two examples the original subjects are acceptable in Chinese, they are not proper in these circumstances as directly translated into Chinese. As for the third one, the original structure of using "it" as a formal subject with the real subject led by "that" put at the end of the sentence never occurs and is never acceptable in Chinese sentence structure. The structure of employing "it" as a formal subject is unique in English structure.

Moreover, unlike what is in Chinese, non-living things or abstract concepts as well as the living beings frequently serve the subjects that can perform actions in English. That is to say, in English sentences, both animate things and inanimate things can be used as the subject exerting certain acts. Those subjects served by non-living things or abstract concepts are the so-called inanimate subjects. Look at the following sentences.

# Chapter Four　The Reflection of CTP in Chinese and English Languages

(1) An idea suddenly struck him.

(2) Nightfall found him many miles short of his appointed preaching place.

(3) His bonhomie often brought him many friends.

(4) Dawn met him well along the way.

(5) Astonishment, apprehension, and even horror oppressed her.

(6) His absence of mind during the driving nearly caused an accident.

In Chinese, however, notions like "idea" "nightfall" "bonhomie" and "dawn" in examples (1) (2) (3) and (4) rarely act as the subjects that perform the behaviors like "strike" "find" "bring" and "meet" in those four examples. In Chinese thought, these things usually function as the objects to undertake these verbs. If they are to put in the place of subjects the passive form has to be employed or the verbs should be changed, whereas the passive form is not so widely and prevailingly used in Chinese for the too much use of it seems awkward and inefficient, the issue of which will be discussed in the next subdivided part. As a result, when such sentences are put into Chinese, certain animate subjects are added to meet the need in Chinese.

In examples (5) and (6), the abstract nouns "astonishment, apprehension, and even horror" and "absence" are used as the subjects to perform the behaviors of "oppress" and "cause", which, in Chinese, is understandable but seems a little strange and thus seldom used in this way. Therefore, other nouns are chosen to replace the original ones. The followings are the suggested translations of the former examples.

(1a) 他突然想起了一个主意。

(2a) 当夜幕降临时,他离预定的布道地点还有好几英里路。

(3a) 在东方欲晓时,他早已走了一大段路了。

(4a) 他为人和善,因而朋友很多。

(5a) 她感到心情抑郁,甚至惊恐不安。

(6a) 他开车时心不在焉,差点出事故。

## 5. Preference of Active Form VS Passive Form

The subjective (personal) consciousness and objective consciousness thought patterns that are preferred respectively in China and the West have a strong influence on the voice of Chinese and English languages.

### 5.1 Preference of Active Form in Chinese

Since Chinese people consider things anthropocentrically, it is very difficult for them to consider man as a predicative or objective existence. Moreover, in Chinese cultural thought patterns the idea of unity and mixture of the animate things and the nature is deeply rooted in people's mind. The active or the passive condition is self-evident and at the same time a little vague, which is no need to be divided so clearly as that in the West. Therefore, the passive voice of the sentence is not well developed in the Chinese language. Even if the passive voice is put to use, it does not take a relatively fixed form like that of English sentences. There are more indicators of the passive voice other than "被" in the Chinese language. In other words, most sentences that convey the passive message are presented in the form of active voice. See the following examples.

大部分问题已圆满解决,只剩下个别次要问题有待讨论。

Most of the questions *have been* settled satisfactorily. Only a few of secondary importance remain to be solved.

整个公园很是安静。小径深处才见到双双情侣。

The park is very quiet. Only deep in a secluded walkway can lovers *be seen* seeking for privacy.

# Chapter Four  The Reflection of CTP in Chinese and English Languages

希望该校党组织迅速解决他的问题。

*It was hoped* that the Party organization of the school would solve his problem without delay.

困难克服了,工作完成了,问题也解决了。

The difficulties *have been overcome*, the work *has been finished* and the problem *solved*.

## 5.2  Preference of Passive Form in English

In western cultural thought patterns, the subject and the object are so clearly divided that the active or the passive condition is distinct. Therefore, in English the passive voice is explicitly and definitely expressed in form while in Chinese it contains the distinction between the explicit one and the implicit one. Sometimes an expression with passive voice in English has to be changed into one with active voice or implicit passive voice in Chinese.

All men are created equal.
人人生而平等。(active)

The glory of the Lord shall be revealed.
上帝的光环再现。(active)

Many voices have been raised demanding the setting up of an Arab common market.
许多人都呼吁建立一个阿拉伯共同市场。(active)

It is a dream deeply rooted in the American dream.
这个梦深植于美国梦之中。(implicit passive)

Every hill and mountain will be made low.
高山夷平。(implicit passive)

Mississippi will be transformed into an oasis of freedom and justice.
密西西比州会改变成为自由和公正的青春绿洲。(implicit passive)

The criminal was executed.
罪犯枪毙了。(implicit passive)

## 6.Spiral Preference VS Linear Preference

### 6.1 Gereral Depictions of Spiral and Linear Preferences

Since Chinese possess indirectness in their thought patterns while the Westerners prefer directness, these particular patterns are also reflected in Chinese and English languages respectively. Among the study in this area, the most famous foreign scholar is Kaplan, who conducted researches into the rhetorical practices of students whose first language was not English. After examining nearly seven hundred English essays written by non-native students, Kaplan published his paper in *Language Learning* entitled "Cultural Thought Pattern in Intercultural Education" (1966). The seven hundred compositions were contrasted with the normal, linear topic development expected by native readers of English. He pointed out, through research, that students from different cultural backgrounds tend to show different ways of putting forward their points of view. Five cultural thought patterns related to five language groups are discussed respectively in his study. Here only two of them are dealt with——English and Oriental.

# Chapter Four  The Reflection of CTP in Chinese and English Languages

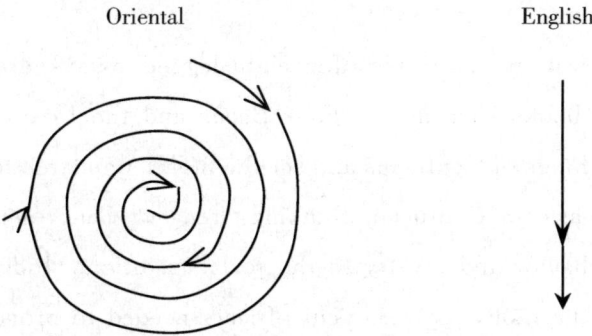

Figure 2    (Kaplan, 1966:15)

Figure 2 is a diagrammatic representation of English and oriental nations. The former diagram in figure 2 is the representation of the Oriental language group including Chinese, Japanese, Korean, Thailand, and so on. "Oriental" group is designated by a circular, spiral and indirect line marked by "indirection". "In this kind of writing, the development of the paragraph may be said to be 'turning and turning in a widening gyre.' The circles or gyres turn around the subject and show it from a variety of tangential views, but the subject is never looked at directly." (Kaplan, 1966) The latter diagram, also the simplest one, represents English language group, which is a vertical straight line with a downward-pointing arrow typifying the linear logical development of the English paragraph.

## 6.2  Spiral Preference in Chinese

In general, Kaplan argued that Chinese as well as other "Oriental" writing is indirect. A subject is not discussed directly but is approached from a variety of indirectly related view. The indirectness in Chinese writing appears as the spiral form, stating one's opinion indirectly like a spiral. This form originated from the "eight-legged essay", an essay form that became the standard device of the civil service examination in the middle of the fifteenth century and survived as an accepted literary form until the early twentieth century. It constitutes the principal framework for Chinese expository and persuasive writing.

The organization and topics for eight-legged essays are derived from classic Chinese books such as the *Four Books* and the *Five Classics*, which convey the teachings of Confucius and set the moral standards for society. Two principles are basic in Confucian thinking: ren, or benevolence; and li, or propriety of behavior and loyalty to the social traditions. Individuals were to maintain social harmony. Government officers needed to prove their skills in social harmony through the writing of the eight-legged essay. It did not allow for much individual self-expression, which is considered socially harmful.

Take thetraditional structure of Chinese essays, that is, four-part model of "qi" "cheng" "zhuan" and "he" as an example. "Qi" prepares the reader for the topic, literally opens the door and not necessarily involves an introduction of the topic; "cheng" introduces and develops the topic, usually with lateral elaboration; "zhuan" turns to a seemingly unrelated subject, showing twists and turns in the arguments and "he" sums up the essay, where the author's opinion is established or hinted. This model is quite popular among the Chinese, as is in the following example.

[起]我们人类是通过说话和书写来相互了解和认识世界的。[承]由此我们知道,交流对于我们认识自我和我们周围的世界是多么的重要。电脑知识对于在当今的世界里有效地进行交流至关重要。[转]每一个人和任何人,不管他或她是教师,大学生,记者,工程师,推销员还是白领职员,都有必要通过与别人交流拓宽自己的世界。电脑知识可以使这种交流进行的更加有效,以达到拓宽世界的目的。[合]因而,在今天的世界,掌握必要的电脑知识具有重要的价值。

The theme of this passage "在今天的世界,掌握必要的电脑知识具有重要的价值" is placed at the end and it is not mentioned either at the beginning part of "qi" or at the middle part of "cheng" or "zhuan". A Chinese reader is accustomed to this pattern of writing while it seems, to a Western reader, lack of logic and confusing in arriving at the conclusion of the theme.

## 6.3 Linear Preference in English

On the contrary, English writing is characterized as beginning with a topic statement, then developing that topic with related ideas supporting it, and at last making a conclusion of the whole essay. Specifically, this linearity begins with uttering the central meaning and then developing gradually to other items either with parallel relations or continuously evolving further items that are derived naturally from the previous ones. Thus, English paragraph development is characterized by linearity, directness, clarity, and logic, which in general, is regarded as the critical criteria for good English writing by natives. Anything different from these characteristics violates natives' expectation and probably can be looked upon as strange or awkward writing performance. Look at the following two examples.

(1) The village of Marlott lay amid the northeastern undulations of the beautiful Vale of Blakemore or Blackmore aforesaid, an engirdled and secluded region, for the most part untrodden as yet by tourists or landscape-painter, though within a four hours' journey from London. (Hardy: Tess of the D'Urbervillers)

前面说过的那个美丽的布雷谷或布莱谷,是一处群山环抱,幽静偏僻的地方,虽然离伦敦不过4个钟头的路程,但是它的大部分不曾有过游历家和风景画家的足迹。马勒村就在它东北部那块起伏地带的中间。

(2) Engels spoke with the authority and confidence, born of forty years closest friendship and intellectual intimacy, during which he had grasped, as no other man had, the full significance of Marx's teachings.

由于40年最亲密的友谊和思想契合,恩格斯对马克思学说的意义比任何人都了解得彻底。他就凭这40年所特有的威望和信心说了这些话。

These two examples in English are typical representatives of English linearity and directness, both of which put the main body "The village of Marlott lay" and "Engels spoke" at the beginning. It is clear that the center or core of a sentence is usually put immediately at the beginning in English. In the English version of example (1), the theme and stressing point "Marlott" is immediately put forward at the beginning of the sentence. Then the sentence is developed from the inward to the outward till the faraway "London" is involved. While the Chinese version begins with the known information "Blakemore or Blackmore", continuously mentions the faraway "London", and then turns back to the nearby "Marlott", the theme of the passage. This is a typical example of spiral thought. In example (2), the condition is similar for the stressing point "Engels spoke" is also directly stated in the English version. But those focusing points are put at the end of their Chinese versions and the reasons and other background conditions are placed beforehand with the intention of conforming to the Chinese custom of expression.

# Chapter Five
# Enlightenment in English Learning and Teaching

## 1. Interference of Chinese CTP with Chinese EFL (English as a foreign language) Learners

Now since the dominant thought patterns in China and the West are different and thought patterns are closely related to the way language is used, it is true that Chinese EFL learners will bring theirtraditionally peculiar way of thinking into their production of English compositions.

It is believed that in English learning of Chinese learners, the Chinese cultural thought patterns will definitely influence the results of learning, which inevitably leads to the appearance of English articles with Chinese thought patterns, and as a result, they will turn out more or less compositions with Chinese mode and structure in English. Thus, the interference of cultural thought patterns arises. This phenomenon, in the research of second language acquisition, is called language transfer. Included in the research on transfer is the study of negative transfer or interference. Here the issue of interference is discussed from syntactic and discourse level respectively.

## 2. Interference with English Sentence Writing by Chinese Learners

Influenced by Chinese cultural thought patterns and Chinese language, Chinese EFL learners will produce the English sentences with Chinese structure and sentence type preference. Further studies of this phenomenon will be reviewed in the following two aspects.

## 2.1 Sentence Structure

The influence of Chinese CTP on the structure of English sentences produced by Chinese EFL learners may be reflected in the following examples.

(1) The old lady was very weak; she could hardly stand up.

(2) Although workers create great wealth for the society, the intellectuals' income is much higher than workers.

(3) On the desk are a few books.

(4) These people he is the most competitive.

(5) Summer is difficult to preserve food.

The five examples and the other sentences with the same structure are common to Chinese EFL learners. To Chinese learners, examples (1) and (2) may seem no problem to understand and some of the learners can not find the problem esp. the beginners. Chinese learners producing such sentences are deeply affected by Chinese synthetic, unitive, intuitive and subjective consciousness thought patterns, which definitely cause the paratactic preference in their English writing. It is evident that the Chinese parataxis definitely influences the English learning for Chinese learners, who are accustomed to Chinese thought patterns and the linguistic structures closely related to them. The examples (1) and (2) produced by Chinese English learners are common in English learning. These two sentences miss the necessary connectors and substitutes, which seems incoherent and ungrammatical to English speakers. The revision has to be made to make them acceptable for English speakers. Here are the revised ones.

## Chapter Five　Enlightenment in English Learning and Teaching

(1a) The old lady was very weak so/and/therefore she could hardly stand up.

(2a) Although workers create great wealth for the society the intellectuals' income is much higher than that of workers.

Examples (3) (4) (5) are typical examples of interference by Chinese topic-comment structure, which is deeply stemmed from Chinese synthetic, unitive, intuitional and subjective consciousness thought patterns. In composing English sentences, Chinese learners still feature topic-comment structure, revealing that this framework is deeply rooted in Chinese learners' mind. The structure is displayed as the following.

(3) <u>On the desk</u>　　<u>are a few books</u>.
　　 桌子上　　　　　有几本书。
　　 topic　　　　　　comment

(4) <u>These people</u>　　<u>he is the most competitive</u>.
　　 这些人　　　　　他最有竞争力。
　　 topic　　　　　　comment

(5) <u>Summer</u>　　<u>is difficult to preserve food</u>.
　　 夏天　　　　很难保存食物。
　　 topic　　　　comment

To English speakers such sentences are ungrammatical and even somewhat absurd since the topics "on the desk" "these people" and "summer" are certain not the subjects from the point of view of logic and grammar. To correct these sentences the subjects of the sentences should be identified first and a proper structure should be established.

For instance, in example (3), "on the desk" obviously functions as the adverbial modifier of place, while the real subject should be the "a few books".

This kind of sentences, which in English is called existential sentences, usually organized by a special structure in English — "there be" structure.

In examples (4) and (5), both "these people" and "summer" function as certain kinds of adverbial modifiers. As in example (4), "he" is evidently the subject, the sentence can be revised as "Among these people he is the most competitive."

And in example (5) the whole structure esp. the subject has to be changed as "It is difficult to preserve food in summer" to make it logical in meaning.

Now look at the following groups of sentences:

A: I saw a plane.

B: A plane came into my view.

我看见一架飞机.

A: The book is too difficult for me to read.

B: The book is above/beyond me.

这本书太难,我读不懂.

A: This very formulation indicates the underlying attitude.

B: This very formulation is indicative of the underlying attitude.

这一说法本身已表明其根本态度.

A: A woman who has fair opportunities and has not an absolute hump may marry whomever she likes.

B: A woman with fair opportunities and without an absolute hump may marry whomever she likes.

一个女人只要不是十分驼背,机会好的话,想嫁给谁就可以嫁给谁.

# Chapter Five    Enlightenment in English Learning and Teaching

A: The pop star appeared on the stage, which caused the audience to stand up and applaud.

B: The pop star's presence on the stage brought the audience to their feet in applause.

这位流行歌星在舞台上出现引起了全场观众起立鼓掌.

For a Chinese EFL learner, the former ones of these pairs of sentences are familiar and easy to imitate, while the latter ones seem hard to imitate and grasp although the meanings are clear and the expressions are more preferred over the former ones by English speakers. This phenomenon is the reflection of Chinese dynamic preference and English static preference.

In order to prove and further analyze this phenomenon, the author illustrates with 60 sample writings from freshmen and sophomores in universities which can be found in the Appendix of this book. It is obviously seen from the sample writings of students that most Chinese students are deeply influenced by traditional Chinese thought patterns. Therefore, their writings reflect students' writing habits and characteristics such as inverting structures and using more verbs in the compositions.

Take a sentence in Sample 41 from the Appendix as one example, "Student-centered teaching helps students to learn knowledge and enhance their learning ability." The sentence has no any grammatical mistakes and is fairly excellent from the point of view of grading teachers. While it is probably more common by English native speakers when it is written as "Student-centered teaching helps the students with their knowledge learning and the enhancement of their learning ability."

Take a look at another example in Sample 31, "On the contrary, after we establish the student-centered classroom, our teaching level will be greatly improved." Students tend to use the subject "we, our..." instead of "it, they, its, their..." or other abstract nouns or third person subjects. Besides, the use of the verb "establish" and "improve" can better be altered by its noun form "establishment" and "improvement". Therefore, the sentence can be more accepted by English native speakers as "On the contrary, after the establishment of the student-centered classroom, the teaching level will lead to a great improvement." Since nouns are more frequently used than verbs in English, it seems better to switch the parts of speech from verbs to nouns in English writing.

Take a look at some more examples of such sentences extracted from the 60 sample writings in the Appendix, which structures obviously review the influence of Chinese thought patterns. Followed each sentence is the suggested revision.

(1) Since the TV was invented, some many industry with TV's invention mushroomed.

(1a) Since the invention of the TV, so many industries with TV's invention mushroomed.

(2) But TV also has disadvantages.

(2a) But there are also some disadvantages for TV.

(3) Universities are gradually realizing the concept of student-centered education.

(3a) The concept of student-centered education is gradually realized in universities.

(4) And I think that education can not only focus on learning.

(4a) And I think that it can not just focus on learning knowledge in education.

## Chapter Five  Enlightenment in English Learning and Teaching

(5) Through the society development, the universities are closely change their teaching ways which is the student-centered teaching.

(5a) Through the development of society, the universities are constantly changing their ways of teaching, which is the student-centered teaching.

English is characterized as the wide use of the nouns, prepositions, adjectives, etc. instead of dynamic predicate verbs to express the actions while Chinese is just on the opposite, which causes the deep impact on Chinese EFL learners, who frequently produce sentences with dynamic predicate verbs and seldom think of using other ways for expression.

### 2.2 Sentence Types

The influence of Chinese CTP on sentence types can be proved by the author's own investigation of some sample writings by Chinese EFL learners. As is reviewed that Chinese EFL learners, especially school and college students, when writing compositions, are frequently advised and encouraged to use more simple and short sentences in order to avoid committing mistakes and get good marks in exams. In order to study this phenomenon, the author of this book investigates the sentence types used in first year and second year students' compositions and finds out that most students in the universities, though have studied English for more than ten years, still show almost all the same preference for simple, short sentences.

Table 1  The percentage of sentence types in Chinese EFL learners' 60 compositions

| samples | total | simple | compound | complex | compound-complex | fragments | comma splice |
|---|---|---|---|---|---|---|---|
| 1~60 | 817 | 521 | 58 | 154 | 14 | 27 | 43 |
| % | 100 | 63.8 | 7.1 | 18.8 | 1.7 | 3.3 | 5.3 |

Notes: 1. Fragments are incomplete sentences which consist of only phrases or dependent clauses that are standing alone and Comma splices are sentences with their constituent independent clauses joined by a comma according to McCrea (1985: 237-245).

2. The subjects are 30 first-year students whose compositions are written for the writing task of their homework on the title "My Views on Student-centered Class", which may be revised several times by students and 30 second-year students whose compositions are written for the writing task of their final examination on the title "TV: A Good Thing or a Bad Thing?" These 60 compositions can be found in appendix.

It is evident from the table that more than half, 63.8%, to be more specific, of all the sentences in the students' compositions are simple sentences. Next come complex sentences, 18.8% of the total, compound sentences, 7.1%, comma splices, 5.3%, fragments, 3.3%, and compound-complex sentences, 1.7%. From the statistics, it is naturally deduced that Chinese EFL learners seem to prefer simple sentences to any other sentence types. Though such preference for simple sentences has nothing wrong in itself, when those sentences are examined in detail, it is obvious that many students fail to link some sentences together by means of transitions, which sometimes are necessary. Here are some examples from the compositions:

(1) There are many different kinds of programs. They are resourceful and interesting.

(2) It may be good for someone. It may be bad to someone else.

(3) And she knows the frailties. She can change them.

(4) They couldn't see a bad thing. But I think a bad thing is also a good thing.

# Chapter Five    Enlightenment in English Learning and Teaching

(5) You must know it. And you think a bad thing is a good thing.

(6) We can know everything happened in the world. Even though we stay at home.

Examples (1) (2) (3) have one thing in common, that is, the sentences in each of them, when made to stand alone, can be connected by applying appropriate connectors to make them closely related in meaning as in the following.

(1a) There are many different kinds of programs, which are resourceful and interesting.

(2a) It may be good for someone and bad for someone else.

(3a) And she knows the frailties. Therefore, she can change them.

There are also someneighboring sentences which are connected with some conjunctions, such as "and" "but" "even though", etc., have been treated as separate sentences and allowed to stand alone as in the examples (4) (5) (6).

(4a) They couldn't see a bad thing, but I think a bad thing is also a good thing.

(5a) You must know it and you think a bad thing is a good thing.

(6a) We can know everything happened in the world even though we stay at home.

Based on the Chinese EFL learners' sentence type preference shown in those 60 compositions, the author of this book considers that it is heavily influenced by the Chinese syntactic style, which finally attributes to the Chinese CTP. Comparatively, in native English writings, the simple types of sentences are not so frequently applied as they are in Chinese EFL learners' writings. It may be proved and shown in the following table, in which native English speakers'10 passages in unit one of *New Concept English*: *Fluency in English* are taken as the samples.

Table 2  The percentage of certain sentence types in native English passages

| samples | total | simple sentences | sentences with linking elements | fragments | comma splices |
|---|---|---|---|---|---|
| 1*～10* | 107 | 40 | 64 | 1 | 2 |
| % | 100 | 37.4 | 59.8 | 0.9 | 1.9 |

Note: Sentences with linking elements refer to compound, complex or compound-complex sentences.

Table 2 shows that native English speakers use more sentences with linking elements—compound, complex or compound-complex sentences (59.8%), which come first in number in their writing. Only 37.4% of simple sentences are produced, about 3 in every 10. This number is relatively small compared with the number of simple sentences produced by the 60 students from China in Table 1, which is 63.8%. This preference of more simple sentences in Chinese EFL learners' writing and more sentences with linking elements (compound, complex or compound-complex sentences) in native English writing can be traced back to the parataxis in Chinese language and hypotaxis in English language as what is discussed in Chapter Four of this book.

Mr. Wang Li, a famous linguist in China, once said: "as far as the structure of sentences is concerned, Western language is ruled by law, and Chinese language is ruled by man." (Chinese Grammar Theory, collected works of Wang Li, vol. 1, p. 35, Shandong Education Press, 1984) Let's take a look at the following example.

# Chapter Five  Enlightenment in English Learning and Teaching

Original version: Children will play with dolls equipped with personality chips, computers with inbuilt personalities will be regarded as workmates rather than tools, relaxation will be in front of smell-television, and digital age will have arrived.

Chinese version: 孩子们将会和配备了个性芯片的玩具娃娃玩耍, 带有内置个性的计算机将被视为工作伙伴而不是工具, 人们将会在气味电脑前休闲, 到这时数字时代就来到了。

This English sentence is a juxtaposition of four independent sentences. The first three sentences all use the simple future tense and the last sentence uses the future perfect tense. The relationship between sentences is clearly expressed by tenses, commas and coordinate conjunctions "and". The Chinese translation is obviously a simple narrative, and the relationship between sentences is completely expressed through the semantics of sentences: the first three sentences can be regarded as juxtaposed relations, and the last sentence represents the result.

Therefore, it can be explicitly seen that English emphasizes structure and Chinese emphasizes semantics.

As English is the language of "rule of law", as long as there are no structural errors, many meanings can often be expressed in a long sentence, while in Chinese, because it is "rule by man", semantics are directly expressed through words. Different meanings are often expressed through different short sentences. It is for this reason that almost 100% of the original sentences in English-Chinese translation questions for the postgraduate entrance examination are long and complex sentences, and the translation into Chinese often becomes many short Chinese sentences or absurd long sentences that do not conform to the habits of Chinese expression. For example:

Original version: Interest in historical methods had arisen less through external challenge to the validity of history as an intellectual discipline and more from internal quarrels among historians themselves.

Chinese translation:人们对历史研究方法产生了兴趣,这与其说是因为外部对历史作为一门知识学科的有效性提出了挑战,还不如说是因为历史学家内部发生了争吵。

The English original sentence is a typical long sentence, which consists of 27 words, without any punctuation marks in the middle, and relies entirely on the grammatical structure to break up the meaning of the whole sentence. "less through…and more from" structure forms a complex adverbial to modify the verb "arisen". In Chinese translation, the important content of "interest" is expressed in an independent sentence, while two different reasons are expressed in different sentences, and the whole sentence is divided into parts. So, it is common that there are more long sentences are in English and more short sentences in Chinese.

In English sentences, not only long modifiers can be used in simple sentences to make them longer, but also clauses can be used to complicate sentences, and these clauses are often connected with the main clause or other clauses through the guide words of subordinates. The whole sentence, though seemingly complex, is considered as a whole. In Chinese, short sentences are preferred, coupled with the relatively loose structure for expression. The clauses in English sentences often become independent sentenced when translated into Chinese.For example:

Original version: On the whole such a conclusion can be drawn with a certain degree of confidence but only if the child can be assumed to have had the same attitude towards the test as the other with whom he is compared, and only if he was not punished by lack of relevant information which they

# Chapter Five　Enlightenment in English Learning and Teaching

possessed.

Chinese version：总体而言,得出这样一个结论是有一定把握的,但是必须具备两个条件:能够假定这个孩子对测试的态度和与他相比较的另一个孩子的态度相同;他也没有因缺乏别的孩子已掌握的有关知识而被扣分。

The two only "if-led" clauses in the original text obviously complicate the whole sentence, but because of the coordinate conjunctions "but" and "and", the logical relationship of the whole sentence is very clear. From the above translation, it can be seen that in order to make the Chinese expression more clearly, the original English sentence can be separated into three sentences in Chinese. This practice leaves the impression that there are no clauses in the translation, with only some different and independent sentences.

In sentences, nouns and prepositions are preferably used in English and verbs are preferably used in Chinese.

In English, there are not only personal pronouns such as "we" "you" "he" and "they", but also relative pronouns such as "that" and "which". In long and complex sentences, in order to make the sentence structure reasonable and meaning clear, and to avoid repetition, many pronouns are often used in English. Although there are pronouns in Chinese, because the structure is relatively loose and the sentences are relatively short, many pronouns can not be used in Chinese, and the use of nouns instead of pronouns often makes the meaning clearer. Please look at the following example：

Original version：There will be television chat shows hosted by robots, and cars with pollution monitors that will disable them when they offend.

Chinese version：届时将出现由机器人主持的电视访谈节目及装有污染检测器的汽车,一旦这些汽车污染超标或违规,检测器就会使其停驶。

It can be seen that for components like subject, object and other noun components, more pronouns are used in English, while more nouns are used in Chinese.

In English the passive voice is more frequently used, especially in English for Science and Technology (EST). Although there are some words such as "被" and "由" in Chinese to indicate that the action is passive, this kind of expression is far less common than the English passive voice. Therefore, the passive voice in English is often transferred into active voice in Chinese translation. Let's take a look at the Chinese translation of a group of commonly used English patterns with passive voice:

It must be pointed out that…

必须指出……

It must be admitted that…

必须承认……

It is imagined that…

人们认为……

It can not be denied that…

不可否认……

It will be seen from this that…

由此可知……

It should be realized that…

必须认识到……

It is (always) stressed that…

人们(总是)强调……

It may be said without fear of exaggeration that…

可以毫不夸张地说……

These commonly used sentence patterns with passive voice belong to idiomatic expressions, which appear frequently in EST. Chinese EFL learners should not only be familiar with the fixed translation of these sentence patterns, but also recognize that many passive sentence patterns in English should be translated into Chinese with active voice. Let's look at another typical example:

Original version: And it is imagined by many that the operations of the common mind can by no means be compared with these processes, and that they have to be required by a sort of special training.

Chinese version:许多人认为,普通人的思维活动根本无法与科学家的思维活动相比,认为这些思维活动必须经过某种专门训练才能掌握。

There are three passive voices used in the original text: "is imagined," "be compared" and "be required", which are translated into Chinese with active expressions:"认为""相比"and"掌握".

Sometimes the subject in English with passive voice needs to be translated into Chinese object in order to be more in line with the Chinese habit of expression. Take the following as an example:

Original version: New sources of energy must be found, and this will take time, but it is not likely to result in any situation that will ever restore that sense of cheap and plentiful energy we have had in the past time.

Chinese:必须找到新的能源,这需要时间;而过去我们感觉到的那种能源价廉而充足的情况将不大可能再出现了。

There is another phenomenon in English that it often changes the way of expressing the same thing or same meaning. For example, when the author uses "I think" to express his or her own ideas for the first, it will be obviously boring if it is repeated for the second time, which can be replaced with expressions such as "I believe" or "I imagine". In contrast, the requirement of changing expressions to express the same meaning in Chinese is not as common as that in English, and many English expressions are accepted to be translated into repetitive expressions in Chinese. Take a look at the following example:

Original version: The monkey's most extraordinary accomplishment was learning to operate a tractor. By the age of nine, the monkey had learned to solo on the vehicle.

Chinese version: 这只猴子最了不起的成就是学会驾驶拖拉机。到九岁的时候,这只猴子已经学会了单独表演驾驶拖拉机了。

Both "tractor" and "vehicle" obviously mean the same thing in the sentence. There are variations in English expressions, but repetitive expressions "拖拉机" are used when they are translated into Chinese.

There are two common sayings in English. One is that "you know a word by the company it keeps", which means if you want to know the meaning, the key depends on the word partner. The second is "words do not have meaning, but people have meaning for them", which means the original words have no meaning, and the meaning goes with how people understand them. It shows that the definition and interpretation of words in the dictionary is dead, while the language in practical use is alive. From the perspective of the original text, this flexible use is an extension of the meaning and usage of words, and in order to accurately understand the extension while translating the original, the translator needs to use the skill of reasoning. For example:

Original version: While there are almost as many definitions of history as there are historians, modern practice most closely conforms to one that sees history as the attempt to recreate and explain the significant events of the past.

Chinese version: 尽管关于历史的定义几乎和历史学家一样多,现代实践最符合这样一种定义,即把历史看作是对过去重大历史事件的再现和解释。

# Chapter Five   Enlightenment in English Learning and Teaching

According to word formation and the interpretation from the dictionary, "recreate" means "重新创造", while in the vocabulary of the English syllabus, there is only the noun "recreation", which means "娱乐,消遣". In this case, it is easily to be translated into "重新创造" or "娱乐". Through examination of the word "recreate" used in the sentence, it is not difficult to find that it contains the object "the significant events of the part". Logically, "major historical events of the past" can not be "recreated" but can be imitated and interpreted. The author obviously extends the meaning of this word, which seems more reasonable to be translated into "再现和解释(imitation and interpretation)" in Chinese.

Besides paying great attention to sentence structure it also prefers ellipsis in English. There are many types of English ellipsis, including noun ellipsis, verb ellipsis, syntactic ellipsis and situational ellipsis. In the coordinate structure, English tends to omit the words that have appeared before, while Chinese often repeats the words omitted in English. For example:

Original version: Whether to use tests, other kinds of information, or both in a particular situation depends, therefore, upon the evidence from experience concerning comparative validity and upon such factors as cost and availability.

Chinese version: 因此,究竟是使用测试,其它种类的信息,还是在特定的情况下两者都使用,取决于关于相对效度的来自经验的证据,同时还取决于成本和可获得性这样的因素。

"Whether…or…" is a coordinate conjunction. The infinitive "to use" is omitted before "or", and the verb "depends" is omitted between "and" and "upon".

There are more examples of ellipsis in English, which, when translated into Chinese, are preferably repeated:

Original version: Ambition is the mother of destruction as well as of evil.
Chinese version: 野心不仅是罪恶的根源,同时也是毁灭的根源。

Original version: Reading exercises one's eyes; Speaking, one's tongue; while writing, one's mind.
Chinese version: 阅读训练人的眼睛,说话训练人的口齿,写作训练人的思维。

Original version: One boy is a boy, two boys half a boy, three boys no boy.
Chinese version: 一个和尚挑水喝,两个和尚抬水喝,三个和尚没水喝。

In the expression of multi-logical thinking, judgment or conclusion often comes first in English, followed by facts or description, that is, the focus comes first, while in Chinese it is from cause to effect, from hypothesis to inference, from fact to conclusion, that is, the center of gravity comes later. Have a look at the following examples:

Original version: I was all the more delighted when, as a result of the initiative of your government it proved possible to reinstate the visit so quickly.
Chinese version: 由于贵国政府的提议,才得以这样快地重新实现访问。这使我感到特别高兴。

Original version: The assertion that it was difficult, if not impossible, for a people to enjoy its basic rights unless it was able to determine freely its political status and to ensure freely its economic, social and cultural development was now scarcely contested.
Chinese version: 如果一个民族不能自由地决定其政治地位,不能自由地保

## Chapter Five    Enlightenment in English Learning and Teaching

证其经济、社会和文化的发展,要享受其基本权利,即使可能,也是不容易的。这一论断几乎是无可置辩的了。

All the previous examples definitely show the distinction between the sentence structures in Chinese and English. Since Chinese language prefers parataxis and English language prefers hypotaxis, which are closely related to Chinese and English CTP, Chinese CTP will undoubtedly influence the Chinese EFL learners' sentence writings in English as well as those in their first language or mother tongue.

### 3. Interference with English Discourse Writing by Chinese Learners

Since Chinese learners grow up under the Chinese cultural background and with the spirit formed under the influence of Chinese CTP, they will naturally create English articles in accordance with Chinese way of thinking, which makes the understanding of their products such a struggle for westerners.

The indirectness and spiral form in Chinese thought definitely influence the English passages written by Chinese students. Kaplan's study in 1966 is a representative, which is discussed in details previously. He notes that non-native students do not write in the way that is expected by natives, that is, what they write is not necessarily wrong in grammar, but it is not idiomatic in terms of discourse requirement. Chinese writer Cai Jigang (2001) points out that specifically, English compositions by Chinese students consistently show evidence of use of either the eight-legged or the four-part or the three-foot organizational patterns, a restricted expression of personal feelings and views, an indirect approach to the chosen topic, and a preference for prescribed, formulaic language, all of which are so unfamiliar to native English-speaking instructors that they mistakenly perceive these students as "poor writers". Take the following sample chosen from the compositions entitled "TV: a good thing or a bad thing?" by the second-year students as an example:

> Recently, TV sets are nearly in each family. Watching TV has become a part of our life. As a media tool, it makes people's life a colorful world.
>
> Through the TV, you could see outside world just sitting at home. You could know what you want to know by using it. And then, TV set can also give people rest. When you feel tired after a whole's day work and study. In the evening, sitting in front of the TV set, watching some interesting programs, listening to some wonderful music. You must forget a whole day's tired. And then, having a sweet sleep, you would work hard tomorrow.
>
> But different people have different ideas. Some of them thought that TV sets would waste much of the time in our life. In fact, there are some people who spend much time in watching TV. They didn't work well. Even making many bad things.
>
> In my view, if you can use TV well, it will bring your life more happiness. So please control yourself, study, work hard and have a good rest.

This composition is a typical one among those written by Chinese EFL learners, the structure of which is common among them. Instead of coming directly into the subject — whether TV is a good or a bad thing, the passage opens with the description of TV's prevailing and importance in people's life. Then, in the second and third paragraphs, the author states respectively the advantages and disadvantages of TV. Not until the last paragraph does the author present his own view about TV. Taken into account that this composition is written during the final exam and the student does not have ample time to further illustrate his point, this piece of writing is not too bad

## Chapter Five  Enlightenment in English Learning and Teaching

from a Chinese teacher's point of view, but the organization of it goes against an English speaker's notion of logic, that is, arguing from premises to conclusions.

Another typical example of writing affected by Chinese CPT also comes from the 60 compositions in the appendix entitled "My Views on Student-centered Class":

*The essence of "student-centered" is a teaching method that changes the focus of teachers' teaching into that of students' learning. In the classroom, teachers can not teach in a regular way, but students can participate in classroom learning happily. Teachers should be "directors", while students are "actors".*

*The traditional teaching evaluation only pays attention to the test scores of students. I think the evaluation of "student-centered" teaching can also be diversified. Students' self-evaluation, students' mutual evaluation and teachers' evaluation; you can also pass the periodic examination, unit examination, mid-term examination and final examination; or more simple question checking, etc. In the process of evaluation, we should pay more attention to positive praise and encourage them to put forward their own ideas, so as to make students become a new generation with thinking, ability and personality.*

*With the change of thought, there will be the change of practice. However, we cannot unilaterally believe that "student-centered" is perfect and "teacher-centered" is worthless. Instead, we should use diversified teaching methods according to the characteristics of the curriculum and the needs of teaching objects, so that students can study happily and master their due knowledge and learning skills.*

Likewise, in this composition the author does not come up with his opinions about the student-centered class directly at the very beginning of the passage. Instead, the author explains what the student-centered class is and how it is operated in the first paragraph. Then, in the second paragraph, the author describes the traditional teaching class and depicts the evaluation of the two modes of teaching classes. Finally, in the third paragraph, the author depicts his views on the student-centered class. The organization of this passage still follows the Chinese thought patterns of indirectness in the process of expressing ideas.

In an English speaker's mind, the opening paragraph of an essay normally announces the writer's central topic and identifies his controlling idea, while the conclusion of an essay usually sums up the writer's earlier ideas or restates his thesis, but apparently the compositions of most students do not live up to an English speaker's expectation.

### 3.1 The Problem of Discourse Conception

Under the influence of the curvilinear (spiral) thinking of their mother tongue, students often do not come straight to the point in their discourse writing, but beat around the bush, often with holding the topic at the end, and some students do not even point out the topic from beginning to end. This kind of English text always makes foreigners confused, just as a vivid simile in Chinese described that reading these kind of passages are just like looking at the clouds and mountains surrounded and covered by fog. Students do not know what to say and can not grasp the main points. Taking the CET-4 composition in December 2011 as an example, the title of which is: Nothing Succeeds Without a Strong Will. For one of the students with higher scores, the first two paragraphs of the sample paper are as follows.

## Chapter Five  Enlightenment in English Learning and Teaching

> *You may have heard the humorous saying "Quitting smoking is the easiest thing in the world. I've done it hundreds of times." Of course, it's funny, but at the same time, it reveals a truth which deserves thinking about deeply.*
>
> *My father is a heavy smoker. It took me a long time to persuade him into giving up smoking and finally he accepted my suggestion. He was determined to do it but after some trials, he failed. I'm clearly aware of the important role a strong will plays in success.*

The article did not make a point at the beginning of the article, but first quoted a humorous joke given in the examination paper in the first paragraph to arouse the reader's thinking. Then, in the second paragraph, the author describes a story in which the author persuades his father to quit smoking, and then points out at the end of this paragraph the theme that strong willpower is necessary for success. This kind of approach of beating around the bush is the representative of the typical spiral thinking of the Chinese people.

However, due to the overall use of the student's wording and sentence patterns that was relatively authentic, but did not start with the topic, for the marking experts as Chinese teachers, it is completely acceptable and is given a relatively high score. Nevertheless, this can not conceal the reality that Chinese students are influenced by Chinese spiral thinking.

Therefore, in the teaching of writing and intensive reading, teachers should timely guide students to understand the linear thinking mode of English discourse, reminding students that they should start with the main points and outline as much as possible in the practice of English writing. It is suggested to adopt the method of coming to the point at the very beginning of the passage and subsequently coming to the specific information to avoid ambiguity in writing.

## 3.2 The Use of Conjunctions

Under the influence of Chinese parataxis thinking, a considerable number of students are unable or not good at using English conjunctions. They often write sentences with semantic connections but isolated forms according to the habits of Chinese thinking in their writing. Although some students have the consciousness of using conjunctions, they often use them improperly, resulting in the misuse of conjunctions. Whether it is due to lack of coherence and cohesion or improper use of conjunctions, such articles make people feel awkward to read. The following is still an example of a sample composition from a CET-4 exam, whose last two paragraphs are:

*The words really touch my heart. I'm very fat. I have keep on losing weight for about ten years though I'm only 20 years old. I always think let losing weight begin from the next meal. So I eat a lot in every "before" meal. What I don't have is a strong will.*

*I think a strong will makes all things easy but without it all things get hard. A strong will makes us keep on what we are doing. Everything succeeds with a strong will.*

There is an obvious lack of coherence and cohesion between the sentences, which is somewhat stiff and loose, not in line with the habit of English discourse expression, and is accompanied by some grammatical problems. If the paragraphs can be slightly changed and with the proper use of conjunctions while correcting grammatical errors, the originally loose and slightly messy paragraphs will be a content with complete form and coherence. The improved paragraphs are as follows.

*The words really touch my heart. Because I'm very fat, I have been trying to keep on losing weight for about ten years*

## Chapter Five  Enlightenment in English Learning and Teaching

*though I'm only 20 years old. However, I always think of beginning losing weight from the next meal, so I eat a lot before each meal. Apparently, what I don't have is a strong will.*

*Therefore, I think a strong will makes all things easy, but without it all things turn to be difficult. As a strong will makes us keep on what we are doing, everything will be successful with it.*

Learning English in a Chinese environment is bound to be disturbed and influenced by the mode of thinking of the mother tongue to a certain extent, which is also the main factor for Chinese students to have many problems in English discourse writing. The unique thinking patterns of English and Chinese are reflected in word formation, sentence patterns and discourse formation in both English and Chinese, so Chinese students' choice of words, sentences and text layout will be influenced by Chinese thinking to a certain degree.

As a result, while teaching English, teachers must appropriately get students infiltrated into the Anglo-American culture, including their distinctive mode of thinking. They should make students understand the characteristics of English sentence patterns and discourse, allowing students to be accustomed to imitating authentic English expressions, and avoiding making English sentences with Chinese sentence structure influenced by Chinese mode of thinking, so as to fundamentally improve students' ability to read and write in English, especially their ability in English discourse writing.

Several years ago, some researchers studied the English writing by Chinese overseas students at colleges and universities in California, U. S. A. and found that though those students had mastered English syntactic structures, they demonstrated inability to compose adequate themes, term papers, theses, and dissertations. Instructors wrote on their papers such comments as: "The material is all here, but it seems somehow out of focus," or "Lacks organization," or "Lacks cohesion".(Hu,1989:159)

Some Chinese scholars also notice that arguments by Chinese students are often delayed, and the narrations and statements used seem unconnected in the eyes of a western reader. The beginning of such kind of writing is like what a Chinese idiom has described as a dragonfly skimming the surface of the water, that is, touching something without going into it deeply. They always linger around the topic, but never enter the theme and sometimes mention it only at the end of the writing.

The Chinese people's spiral preference and the westerners' linear preference in their respective native writing has been discussed in particular in part six of Chapter Four, which are deeply related to the indirectness thought in China and the directness thought in the West as it is talked about in part six of Chapter Three. To a Western reader, articles by Chinese lack argumentative coherence because of its reliance on appeals to history, tradition, and authority and its frequent references to historical and religious texts as well as proverbs sometimes. Some phrases, sayings, and allusions, used with the purpose of ornamenting and enlivening the discourse, seem distractive to the Western readers.

## 4. Suggested Ways of Reducing the Interference by Chinese CTP and Chinese Language

At the primary stage of learning, it is no wonder that the influence of Chinese thought patterns attributes a lot to the occurrence of many language errors by Chinese students, who depend heavily on Chinese thought. It seems that it is impossible for English beginners to eliminate the influence of Chinese thought. Strictly speaking, influence from Chinese thought patterns can never be avoided completely unless one is thoroughly blended with the English society. But it can be decreased to the minimum extent through the effort from both the learners and the teachers. The following are some of the suggested

# Chapter Five  Enlightenment in English Learning and Teaching

ways by the author of this book.

For Chinese EFL learners, they should not just wait for teachers to instill the information about the Western cultural knowledge and thought preference into their brains. It is essential for them to play an active role in their learning. Every opportunity should be utilized and created to practise their listening, speaking, reading, and writing abilities. Besides, imitation and translation are both very critical in the process of learning a foreign language.

Firstly, in the process of language input, listening and reading are both the important ways of obtaining the language and function as the leading skills in language learning. Here the author of this book focuses on the development of reading ability, from which the learners can acquire a large number of information including the Western customs and thought. Only by reading a lot can a student learn to speak and write well, which are the essential parts in language output. So, all the students are encouraged to read as much as possible the English writings by native English writers in particular. By reading, they can get the exact meaning of some words and familiarize themselves with some useful sentence structures. At the same time, students may acquire many customary expressions and collocations without being forced to memorize what is right or wrong and what is acceptable or unacceptable.

It is also necessary to note that selecting proper materials is rather critical for reading. The selection of the materials should match the level and degree of the readers. From the author's own teaching and learning experience, there are two basic principles in choosing materials. For one thing, the materials should not be too difficult or too easy compared with the readers' own level in reading. For another, the materials should not be restricted within a certain field or style, that is, a wide range of materials are supposed to be chosen to broaden the readers' horizon.

To English beginners and English learners at comparatively lower level, materials for native children, for example, some encyclopedias for children or junior, or revised articles from native ones are more suitable because of their simplicity and easiness. To learners at mediate level or higher, some English originals, newspapers and magazines, for instance, *Reader's Digest*, can be selected to meet their needs.

After selecting the proper materials, one should consider the question of how to read. Reading is generally divided into intensive reading and extensive reading, both of which are essential in improving one's ability to grasp English.

For English self-learners, intensive reading means selecting the passages, chapters, sections, paragraphs or sentences one prefers to read in great detail so as to read aloud and memorize.

As for extensive reading, one may choose various kinds of reading materials to read, which allows no precise understanding and careful learning but requires grasping the general idea at a relatively rapid speed. Both of the two kinds of reading contribute to the acquisition of unadulterated English, which contains much useful knowledge that is helpful to the comprehension and grasp of English CTP.

Secondly, after enough English reading, learners should turn to some practical work — imitating the word choice, sentence structure and even the language style of the natives. In this way, they express their ideas directly in English thought patterns and not in the way of translating Chinese into English. So, the influence of Chinese thought can be diminished gradually. As it is pointed out in *American English Rhetoric* (Robert G. Bander, 1983) that even though English thought patterns, sentence structures and discourse arrangement are not native to non-native learners, once they understand them, they can more easily imitate them. By doing so, learners will succeed in writing more effective English and become more accustomed to the English way of organization and expression.

Thirdly, translation is another good way ofpractice, which will be helpful

# Chapter Five   Enlightenment in English Learning and Teaching

in illuminating the cultural differences in language use. It is a useful tool to make learners conscious of the different ways in which languages and their related cultures encode experience. As the effect of these ways is gradual and not obvious during a short period of time, Chinese learners need to be patient enough to practice reading, imitation and translation.

Finally, in addition to the practice through the process of language input and output, Chinese EFL learners should also familiarize themselves with the Chinese and English cultural traditions and thought patterns by intentionally contacting them, directly or indirectly. They should pay more attention to the development of their cross-cultural consciousness and sensitivity.

For educators, a working knowledge concerning linguistic and cultural differences between English and Chinese is necessary, which will enable them to provide EFL learners with informationand knowledge expected to possess by native English speakers. It has been noticed that teachers are more concerned with sentence-level accuracy when teaching writing than with units larger than the sentence as well as with explanation and discussion of organization and writing style of a passage. This is because many teachers in China feel that the most serious problem with Chinese EFL learners, in meeting the requirements of national English examination in writing, is incorrect English usage mainly including the choice of words and the sentence structure, so that their main objective is to teach the students how to write grammatically correct sentences with proper words in English, and consequently much time and effort are spent in teaching grammar rules and vocabulary.

However, teachers should, in the meantime, know that particular options, which are considered odd by English speakers, are not random or only due to learners' misuse of certain English grammar rules, but may come as a result of linguistic and cultural constraints not necessarily shared by native English speakers. That is, Chinese EFL learners sometimes make mistakes because they do not know the cultural differences esp. the distinct cultural thought patterns between China and the West and the linguistic differences between Chinese and English. Therefore, the teachers should be equipped with a working knowledge of linguistic, rhetorical and cultural differences between English and Chinese, which will help them increase Chinese EFL learners' cross-cultural awareness. It should be noted that a teacher is not simply a grammar or a language teacher, but should at the same time be a cross-cultural interpreter and communicator.

As forinputting the cultural knowledge and increasing cross-cultural awareness, the educators or teachers propose various ways through their experience and study. For example, they can organize some talks and lectures on the concept of culture and on differences in customs and living habits. Besides, playing English films and videotapes is another vivid and effective way to introduce western customs and cultures. In addition, contacting native English speakers and studying western culture and literature to learn about cultural information are all the helpful and suggested ways. By these different approaches, the Chinese EFL learners will gradually understand and familiarize themselves with the western CTP, which is of great importance in their English learning.

Due to the huge differences between Chinese and English and between Chinese culture and the culture of English-speaking countries, many teachers and learners in China think that the effect of negative transfer of Chinese, their mother tongue, is greater than that of positive transfer. Therefore, when exploring the influence of mother tongue, researchers often focus on the negative effects of mother tongue and advocate avoiding mother tongue interference in the process of learning English.

Some educator sadvocate that learners try not to use their mother tongue in class in order to create a pure language environment so as to learn a foreign language in the way that they have grasped their mother tongue. It seems that

## Chapter Five  Enlightenment in English Learning and Teaching

this can, to a large extent, get rid of the influence of mother tongue and avoid the so-called pidgin or interlanguage. They assume that in this way learners may make few or no language mistakes at all and learn a purer and more authentic foreign language.

However, is it the truth to learn English efficiently as simple as just rejecting the mother tongue? It is generally accepted that language and thinking are inseparable, where thinking is the foundation of language, and language is the carrier of thinking. Although it is still not sure what the mechanism of children's mother tongue acquisition is, one thing is clear, that is, it must be done on the basis of normal thinking ability.

It is self-evident that children will definitely think in their mother tongue after they have acquiredit. As Butzkamm, a professor of English teaching in Germany, puts it in a good analogy: "the mother tongue is not a coat, and learners can take it off and throw it out before stepping into the foreign language classroom." Therefore, mother tongue transfer can never be underestimated, whose existence must be admitted. It must not be denied that mother tongue transfer not only interferes with foreign language learning, but also has its positive effect. In a way, it can also help students learn a foreign language well.

The process of learning is not just to make students master specific knowledge and skills of one or several subjects or disciplines, but also to make students learn how to learn, that is, to master the knowledge and skills of learning methods. Learning methods can be regarded as the learning experience, which can produce a wide range of general transfer to the subsequent learning practice. Therefore, in English teaching process, teachers should not only teach students the knowledge, but also make them master the necessary skills to learn the knowledge through certain types of practice.

Firstly, thecomparative practices (such as judging the right and wrong, correcting mistakes, etc.). Teachers put forward some error-prone sentences made by students as key points for targeted comparative analysis, so as to help students improve their ability of discrimination.

Secondly, selective practices (such as multiple choice, word selection and blank filling, etc.). They are mainly some exercises specially compiled to improve students' ability of analysis and judgment, so as to eliminate students' ambiguous or confused understanding of some knowledge.

Thirdly, intensive practices (such as essay question, specialized training for listening, speaking, reading and writing, etc.). It is characterized by intensity of training and repeated practice of a language project in a short period of time in order to master it for proficiency.

Fourthly, heuristic exercises (such as completing the dialogue, looking at the picture and talking about the topic, prompt compositions, topic discussions, etc.). The main purpose of this kind of practices is to train students to search for more than one solution of the problem. It is aimed to train students to think more from multiple angles and to integrate the ideas according to the needs of real communication, so as to further cultivate students' scientific way of thinking and form good thinking habits, and thus to improve the effectiveness of teaching.

Through the various forms of practices talked above, teachers can guide students to use their knowledge spontaneously and voluntarily to overcome the negative transfers and promote the positive transfers of the first language.

# Chapter Six  Conclusion

Since language and thought are interrelated to each other and simultaneously interactwith each other, both of which are closely attached to culture, the thought patterns of the people from different cultural traditions will definitely be revealed in their culturally transmitted languages. This is specifically described and discussed in the previous chapters. The diverse CTP presented in Chapter Three, their reflection in Chinese and English languages noted in Chapter Four, and the Chinese CTP's interference with EFL learning contained in Chapter Five are all worthy of consideration and focus for Chinese EFL learners and teachers.

Meanwhile, attention should also be paid to the fact that in the human history there is a distinction between different periods of time, according to which people's ways of thinking constantly vary. To mention this, it does not mean to deny, but to recognize the fact that in every nation there are special thought tendencies, which have persisted throughout these historical stages. The more communication progresses, the closer the connection between nations becomes. The more the world becomes unified, the less the disparity of ways of thinking among nations will be, and the slighter in degree will CTP interference function in EFL learners' sentence structures and discourse writing.

It is essential to reaffirm that despite all the contrastive cultural thought patterns the human thoughts have something in common, which is the basis for mutual understanding between different nations, or there will be no possibility for the inter-cultural communication. However, though today the world is becoming a global village and Chinese as well as westerners are learning from each other, the distinctions between Chinese and the western thought patterns will still be present for a relatively long time.

It should also be pointed out that although the western CTP are mentioned in this book as a systematic group, there undoubtedly exist distinctions in particular thought preferences between different nations within the western group. It is only that these distinctions between different western nations, which grow up under the same or similar cultural traditions, do not seem to differ so widely compared with those between the Chinese group and the western group, which are from largely diverse cultural traditions. In this book the western CTP mostly refer to the CTP of English-speaking nations represented by Britain and America. The distinctive expressions and structures in English and Chinese languages indicate the dissimilarity and peculiarity of thought patterns of the different nations.

In Chinese EFL learning, problems frequently occur for various reasons. Generally speaking, in second language acquisition, the major mistakes made by learners can be roughly divided into two aspects. One is generally accepted as the developmental error, which is similar to those made by children acquiring their mother tongue. The other is made by the interference of their native language apparently, which is further traced back to the interference of their cultural thought patterns. Chinese learners should carefully study both the diverse expressions and the distinctive cultural thought patterns between the different nations. To help the learners prevent interference from Chinese traditional thought patterns is still such a big task for language teachers in China that continuous and persistent effort should be made on it.

The main purpose of thebook is to inspire some enlightenment for the

## Chapter Six  Conclusion

improvement of English teaching and learning, as well as to provide some useful information and insights for those who are interested in the studies of CTP and communication between the two national groups. It is expected that the book can be of some value and assistance to Chinese foreign language teachers and EFL learners, as well as those who are interested in this aspect of research and study. The contrastive studies of cultural thought patterns in this book is of some help in enhancing one's understanding of various cultural traditions.

There still remains a lot of unsolved issues that are open for discussion and further research. For example, some other contrastive thought preferences between China and the West are to be explored, discussed, studied and systematically classified. The relationship and interaction between the contrastive cultural thought patterns need further discussion and study. Moreover, how can Chinese EFL learners effectively avoid the influence of Chinese CTP is also a significant issue to both the language teachers and learners. It is just an elementary and tentative study towards this field and further empirical study is needed for modification and improvement.

# Appendix

Notes: The following samples extracted from the 60 university students including 30 compositions of the sophomores (samples 1～30) and 30 compositions of the freshmen (samples 31～60) are made no major correction except that of possible spelling mistakes and that of some grammatical errors that will hinder the understanding of the compositions.

**Sample 1:**

Nowadays more and more people tend to watch TV at night, or even watch them in day time, especially in holidays. TV is so close to our daily life. But have you think of this: Is TV a good thing or a bad thing?

Most people may think that TV is good. Because it can bring the information for you even if you just stay at home. You don't have to go anywhere. Further more, it doesn't only bring you the sound but also the vision. It's so convenient. Besides the news, we also can watch some films, plays and so on for fun. So, how good TV is!

But on the other hand, there are also some programs that are not suitable for children, for example, the scene of sex, violent fights and so on. And if the children are too interested in TV, it may bring bad effects to their study.

So, if you enjoy the TV in a proper way, it will do good for us. Don't abuse it! So it may become our friends.

**Sample 2:**

Recently, TV has played more and more important role in our modern life. We benefit a lot from this kind of machine. However, the disadvantages that the TV are bringing to us can also be seen in our life.

For one thing, TV is a good thing which can enlarge our eye-sight. While we needn't go out of our doors, we can obtain information of all over the world from TV. Watching TV is also a kind of relaxing. After a busy day, listening the music and watching the film from a TV can be the best way to comfort our tiring boy. However, TV also has bad effect on us. Watching TV can make some troubles to our eyes. And it is unhealthy for our body. Besides, the violence films may corrupt the spirits of young children.

In my opinion, one coin has two sides. We should take good advantage of TV to enrich our life. And we also have to get rid of the disadvantages the TV brings us.

**Sample 3:**

Nowadays, nearly every family in the world has a TV set. Watching TV becomes one part of our daily life. But there is debate that TV is a good thing or a bad thing.

Some people think that TV is beneficial for us. They believe that we can get many useful information from the TV program and we can get recreation from some TV plays. Watching TV is a kink of means of enjoying ourselves. But others do not think so. They contend that there are many violence and sex in the TV plays and movies. These are opened to the children. It is not favorable for their health.

In my opinion, each coin has two sides. TV has its merits and demerits. It depends on how to use it. The best way of using it is that we should not drive ourselves too much on it and get what we want.

**Sample 4：**

Everything has two sides, a good side and a bad thing. In my opinion, whether a thing is a good thing or a bad thing, is depending on its sue for people.

We can't say a thing must be a good thing or must be a bad thing, for everything has two sides. For example, most of people watch TV everyday. We say TV is a good thing is because it can bring me some lately news about political, goods and so on. But we can also say TV is a bad thing. Because some programs will teach children some bad things. Some children do some dangerous things like the film in TV that lead them to die. So we can't say TV is a good thing or a bad thing.

In short, everything has its advantages and disadvantages. Depending on its advantages it is a good, depending on its disadvantages it is a bad thing. So I think everything is a good thing and also a bad thing.

**Sample 5：**

In my opinion, TV is a bad thing although the TV has become an important thing in our modern life.

First, it hurt badly our eyes. Because the programs on TV are interesting, they attracted many children. So the children spend more time watching, and after a long time, their eyes will be hurt badly.

Second, more and more advertisements put on TV now . But some of them deceive people to buy and some people cheated. Sometimes, the result of buying these false things are serious bad. For example, the false milk can kill many babies, the false wine can kill people. But some false milk and wine advertisement can be watched on TV.

Third, the TV influence our study. When we watch TV, we can't spend more time studying. So the scores of the study will be fewer and fewer.

So, the TV is a bad thing. We should spend fewer time on TV than before.

**Sample 6:**

As we know our world has changed very large. Everyday, every hour, every minute will have change. The world is very mysterious. But our life circle is very small. We can't know everything quickly. So I think TV can help us solve this question.

In my opinion, as an university student we should know everything, but even not every at least we should know that happen in our country. So I think program about news is very useful and it is very popular in our common life. And the second program I like is about sports, because I like basketball very much. So I think this will help we know more and more superstar. That is wonderful thing in my life. The third I think is music. I know one idiom. "No music, no life". That's great. If no TV, I can't look singers sing the song on the platform. That's a pity.

So to conclude my opinion, TV made my life happiness and from it I know lots of things, so I think TV is a good thing.

**Sample 7:**

As is known to us, TV plays an important role in our modern life. But it has both advantages and disadvantages. It depends on people's interest. In my opinion, TV is a good thing. In other words, it has more advantages than disadvantages.

First of all, as a kind of medium, it supplies very much information that is necessary and essential for people. We may know information of commodities, market and so on. Without it, our life would be uncomfortable, and many problems will happen. Then, it becomes a part of life. In spare time, we can regard TV as a manner of recreation. TV provides us with movies, new and something strange and interesting, which makes our life full and varied.

People's awareness improves and attaches more and more importance to the advantages of TV. So we can say it is a good thing.

**Sample 8:**

What TV actually brings us? All of us know that almost every family has one or more TVs. When we meet each other we should talk TV programs. So we can say TV has gone into our daily life. Although it so popular, I still issue that TV remains both some good things and some bad things.

First, TV can provide us a lot of information all over the world. Second, when we return home form work time we can relax us by watching TV. The last we can study by TV but not go to school.

But, there always some bad things for it. For example, more and more unhealthy things for children began to appear on it. And children like watching TV too long time on the weekend ever on holiday. It is bad for their body healthy.

In a word, the good have more weight than the bad. So we should watch TV in proper time and refuse to see those unhealthy things.

**Sample 9:**

Now, more and more families have TV set and a lot of people like watching TV. But very a little people thought one problem, TV, a good thing or a bad thing. On a certain sense, I think TV is a good thing.

First, long time ago, there was no TV, the news spread very slow, and if you want to know something you had to ask a lot of people. But now if you want to know what happened yesterday in your country, you can watch TV. Second, if you want to buy something but you don't know which is fit for you, you can watch TV. There are a lot of advertisements. You can choose the best one. Third, when you felt lonely and didn't know what things you can do, you can watch TV. There are some movies on the TV.

Generally speaking, I think TV is a good thing. Watching TV when you felt lonely, you will find something interesting.

**Sample 10:**

In our lives, I think it happens many things. And they include good things and bad things.

In fact, people wish to happen a good thing to themselves. They wouldn't see a bad thing. But I think a bad thing is also a good thing. For example, one person didn't pass the examination, she failed. People think it was so bad. Because she wasn't a good student. Is it right? No. because she actually see some the weaker ones passed the examination. And she knows the frailty. She can change them. From then on, she change the better one. She is a good student and no longer failed. Isn't is a bad thing? So a bad thing is encouraged by yourself. You must know it. And you think a bad thing is a good thing.

So a bad thing is also a good thing.

**Sample 11:**

I think the TV is the most great invention of the 20th contrary. It is a very useful and good thing. In a certain sense, TV has changed the lives of modern people.

First, TV can transfer information to where has a TV. Its speed of transferring is very fast and it can convey picture. During the radio and newspaper, you only can listen or read, you can't see the screen. Second, TV made our lives exciting. We can see a film by the TV, know some knowledge from it. Because of TV, we can know some things of other places or other countries. We can see a sport game from kilometers away, but 100 years ago, that was impossible.

Of course, everything has the two sides. TV also has some disadvantages.

For example, there are a lot of bad games in TV.

In my opinion, TV plays an important role in our lives now. it help us to know news, knowledge. It make us happy and exciting. In one word, TV is a good thing.

**Sample 12:**

As far as we know, every coin has two sides. The same is true with the TV. TV is one of most effective media, which transmit information and things, happening around or out the sight of us. But it also bring some "garbage" to us. I prefer to say, if we take advantage of TV, TV is a good thing.

First, TV can broaden our mink. It can tell us so many views and knowledge we can't get ourselves. Second, TV improve the communication between the countries which are far from each other. People could record their film of life and sent it to the others, with the help of TV. Last but not the least, TV made our life more colorful. Since the TV was invented, some many industry with TV's invention mushroomed. Such as, the advertisement industry and the program for enjoyment.

Jin spite of a few disadvantage of TV. TV take so much comfortable and convenience to us. Our life could not live colorful without TV.

**Sample 13:**

Following the developing of the society, TV becomes more popular in the life. People watch TV every day. It's indispensable for living. I think TV is a good thing.

First, TV is a useful machine. There are something interesting or important every day. Everyone should know the news. So TV is benefit. If you want to know many news, you can use TV. Then you can know news quickly and truly and you can learn so many knowledge. Second, TV is a easy machine. You need not buy newspaper or magazine. Sometimes, if you buy them later, you will lose many news and delay something. So you can use TV. It's easy to use, the news is quickly. Third, TV will make you at ease. Every day when you return home from working or learning, you will feel so tired. At this time, you can watch TV. There are many different kinds of programs. They are resourceful and interesting. You will feel relax. TV make your life resourceful.

On the whole, TV is a useful machine. It makes you learn news or knowledge and you will feel relax by it. So TV is a good thing.

**Sample 14:**

TV is a new invention during the 19th century. Sometimes it's a good thing, but sometimes it's a bad thing.

The invention of TV is open the sight of eyes of man. It can make man know lots of things by it. Such as the senses of all the world, the politics of other countries, the sports, and so on. Man's life may become much more wonderful. For example, my old sister, she learnt English by TV. There's a lecture about English, she watch it everyday. Now she can speak English well. But TV is also a bad ting. Now every family has one child. He or she stays at home after the class or on holiday, may not do homework. Instead they watch TV. It can delay their education. And sometimes the ads in the TV are not suitable for the children, even harmful to them, which may teach them some bad things. There are so many examples about this.

The TV is a good thing or a bad thing, I think nobody can tell it certainly. We must divide it by myself.

**Sample 15:**

Recently, TV sets are nearly in each family. Watching TV has become a part of our life. As a media tool, it make people's life a colorful world.

Through the TV, you could see outside world just sitting at home. You could know what you want to know by using it. And then, TV set can also give people resting. When you feel tired after a whole day work and study. In the evening, sitting in front of the TV set, watching some interesting programs, listening some wonderful music. You must forget a whole day's tired. And then, having a sweet sleep, you would work hard tomorrow.

But different people have different ideas. Some of them thought that TV set would waste much of the time in our life. In fact, there are some people who spent much time in watching TV. They didn't work well. Even making many bad things.

In my view, if you can use TV well, it will take your life more happiness. So please control you self, study, work hard and have a good rest.

**Sample 16:**

Everyday we watch TV and now TV is necessary in our life. A report says that there're 80% of people would watch TV for one hour a day. In my opinion TV is a good thing.

First, TV can make our life more colorful. Besides playing many other games, such as playing basketball, football and so on. We could watch TV during our free time. It can make our life more interesting. Second, TV can broaden our mind. There're many different kinds of programs on TV and some of them are on other countries of the world. We'll learn many things about the history, custom of the other countries. The third, we can learn more knowledge form TV. Some of the TV program are on the subject of science, math, art and so on. If we are interested in any of them, we can learn it by ourselves.

In one word, TV is a good thing. If we could control the time spending on watching TV, we could find that the world is very colorful and we'll felt very happy with learning more and more knowledge.

**Sample 17:**

In modern economic era, TV in most family becomes an important thing. By increasing TV sets, many problems are present. Some one think TV is bad and others think it is good.

In my opinion, I think TV is good for our life. From TV you can know a lot of things and learn many things. Someone may say you also can know when you read newspaper or listen to radio, maybe you don't know when only listen or read you lonely can remember 35% to 55% of the information. But if you listen and look you may remember 80% of it. From TV you also can learn more information. You can see somewhere where you never could go, and know the latest news. There are many things you can learn or know from TV. I think TV is gook.

Maybe some bad things are played on TV, but it must be little. By human promising and world developing, much more news will be played on TV. Remember when you watch TV you can learn well and quickly.

**Sample 18:**

The invention of TV set have greatly changed our life. TV brought us a lot of benefits, but meanwhile, it also gave us some troubles.

According to the TV programs, we can learn a lot of things of other countries. For example, I am a Chinese. I haven't been to America, but I know the President of America's name is G. W. Bush in 2001. How can I know it, of course I know it from TV. The weather is changing every minutes, but now we can know what is the weather tomorrow through Weather Report on TV. From TV, we can know plenty of significant new in the world every day. TV widens our sight.

But TV also can produce some noise. At midnight, if there was a football game, I would disturb my parents when I was watching it. TV programs can bring some unbenefit influents as well, such as sex, killing, frightening and so on. Are not good at the children's growing.

Everything has two different influent. TV is not out of this rule.

**Sample 19：**

With the life of people developing, TV has become the best normal thing in our family. When we came back home, everyone would watch TV. No matter who he is a dope or a child.

We don't ensure watching TV is a bad thing or a good thing. Every coin has its two sides. When we watch TV we can learn form some useful thing that teach us how to get along with people. Further more, we can learn about the information that we don't know in the realization life. It can make our life become interesting. Watching TV is also a life. But with the program of the TV developing, more and more program are bad for the children's mentally and healthy. These children like to study the thing that they look from the TV. So it take the bad influences to the children.

So watching TV is an unsure thing. It may be good for someone. It may be bad to someone else. We should face the problem rightly and indicate the children to the right forward.

**Sample 20：**

Now every family has a TV set at least. Most of the people would rather like watching TV than movie. Especially children like cartoon channel most of all.

There are some advantage points in watching TV. First, when we are watching TV we can get new and fast information at short time, it can help us make right judgment. Then, children can learn some knowledge from TV, there are more and more educational games in the TV. Third, when some one feels lonely, TV can help him and makes him happily. But TV has its frailty to human health. Many persons must wear glasses because they watch TV too much. And little children also like to watch TV that forget to finish their homework.

In my opinion, if we watch TV fittingly and suitable, TV may become our sufficient friends. It can help us on many ideas. So use the TV in the best way.


**Sample 21:**

With the whole world developing, TV becomes close to our lives. But just as everything in the world, it also has it's own advantages and disadvantages.

We say TV is a good thing because it not only provides a way for relaxation, but also affords us a mean to learn other thing. We can see the things happened at other place. We can enjoy the sight of some other places. May be we can't go. We can know the world not only by hearing but also by seeing.

But as every coin has two sides. Sometimes we also can say it a bad thing. Becuase it is interesting, so many people, expecially many children spend too much time on it. People watch TV after meal immediately, even some watch TV as soon as they get up in the morning. It wastes so much time and becomes bad for our health. So everyone should learn to use it properly.


**Sample 22:**

Recent years, TV can be seen in every family. And most modern people can't live without TV. Is this appearance good or bad? I think every thing has tow sides.

TV has many advantages for modern people. For example, we can learn many things from it.

We can know everything happened in the world. Even though we stay at home. In a modern world, it's very important. We could know the weather, the economic, the news, and so on easily. But it has another thing at the same time. The more we relied on TV, the less we touch other people. Do you see this appearance. Twenty years ago. People get very well relationship with each other. but now. The neighbors seems strongly. Because many people watch TV after work instead of touching other thing.

Different people have different views. If you can used TV as a good way. It must be a good thing. In opposition, it may be a bad thing.

**Sample 23:**

Since the TV set was invented, it changed our lives a lot. At first, it was amazing for all around the people. When we finished our work, we would watch it for resting.

But today, the TV became a war. Some many programs, the watchers aren't satisfied with just watching, they will choose the program which they are interested in. So there's a war between the TV shows. And, every family has a TV set and have child. How long is most suitable for children watching TV. What TV show is fit for the child. Too much blood, or some show just for the other, does it change the children's clear world? It's a war between the parents and the TV. Of course, we can not say that TV is absolutely good or bad. The children will study much more through watching the TV. They can see many other beautiful places which they couldn't be. They can learn many useful knowledge which the actors are animals. Everything has a degree. How to control the degree is a problem which is really hard to do. So what we can do is, to control it as well as possible.

That TV is a good or a bad thing still is a question. Anyway, watching TV in a short distance or in too long time are bad. Remember these.

**Sample 24:**

Nowadays, with the development of the science, our life have changed so swiftly. We have many choices in our spare time. Watching TV is one of the best choices. But it is also the topic that many people have argued with it: Is watching TV a good thing or a bad thing? In my opinion, it is a quite good thing of us.

I certainly have my reasons. First, it is our basic reason: for entertainment. When we are watching TV programs, we relax our selves and put ourselves at ease. The second, we can widen our knowledge. We can just sit in the sofa to see the things in the other side of the earth. We can see all kinds of things on the small box. The third, we can watch the special programs for our hobby, such as music, arts or the sports. But, on the opposite, watching TV also has its frailties. For example, spending too much tie watching TV may affect our normal study and work. It will also do harm to our eyes.

After all, I think that watching TV is a good thing although it has some bad points. But we can regulate our time in watching it. Only when we watch it properly can it be a quite good thing.


**Sample 25:**
While the economic is developing fast in jour society, TV for us is no longer a unfamiliar thing. But it still has many problems for us, esp. the young pioneers.

For one thing, we can't touch the would without TV. We get many views, scenes, political news and so on from it. It really helps us open our eyes. We can catch the rhythmical of the world. It was wided to the most countries too. The other, when the big festival comes we can't live happily and pleasant without the program in it. It brings us the happiness, for the whole family should sit together to watch it. In our daily life everyone is busy all the time. You know, before I think it is a good thing.

But our parents are all afraid that, the programs in the TV brings the bad views and unhealthy things for their children. Very badly effect their children's mental. I want to say TV is a popular electricity production for this world. We should give the open opinions for it. The right education parents for their children should be raised. Let their children know what is right, what is wrong. But not only forbid their children that TV is a bad thing and required them not touch it.

So in my opinion, TV is a good thing. We should change our mind on some problems to know that. Everything has two opposite matter. We can't for one matter perish it all.

**Sample 26:**

Nowadays, the topics, such as, "Have you seen the soap-opera last night?", become more and more prevalent. We can see how important TV plays a role on people's daily life.

TV can benefit our lives in many aspects. Firstly, with the rapid development of cross-cultural and the highly quality of TV programs, every people could appreciate during the TV time. TV can widen people's eye-sight. We can stay at home to make acquaintance with lots of interesting things on TV. What an amazing thing! Secondly, many chain-films are thrived recently. Producer4s tried their best to produce more amusing stories to give their audience. It makes people's life more interesting. Thirdly, people can obtain lots of new around the world at home on the TV. It's benefit to help them to become judicious. Finally, most manufactures make the best use of TV to address many das to introduce their products.

However, just like every coin has two sides, we should consider some bad influential results. First, thriving of the TV's chain-films takes up much time. Second, lots of people enjoy TV so much that they nearly don't want to communicate with each other. what a baffling change! Third, some bad TV products will play a bad role during the young audience healthy growth. At last, long time before TV, the radiation of TV will endanger people's health.

In conclusion, TV is almost a good thing during our lives if we make best use of it and avoid its bad elements.

**Sample 27:**

If someone ask you which part is good and which part is bad of the TV. How could you answer? Do you think it is good or bad thing? Maybe sometimes you like it, put sometime you even want to throw it out. What do you think about it?

In my opinion, first TV is a development. It shows the science and the economy's development. Second, it change our lives widely and deeply. Fore example some years before we just listen to the radio but cannot see the picture. But now you can know the news which happened just a few minutes. It is convenient, interesting and useful. It is good for your career and your life. Every coin has two sides. It also brings some bad parts. For example, it is bad for people's eyes and skin. It waste time and so on.

TV is a mirror history. It makes our lives easy and interesting. Meanwhile, it gives some bad one. I think just control ourselves and use more its good part. We will have good lives.

**Sample 28:**

In the modern world TV spread quickly. I think every family will have it. But is it a good a thing or a bad thing? I think it is a good thing.

First, it can make our sight widely. Because we can't have enough money and time to go abroad. But we want to know other countries' culture, at this time we can use TV to accomplish it. We needn't go out to appreciate. We can only stay at home.

Second, we can get lately information. Everyday we can use the TV to see the news report. In this way, we can get a lot of information around us or some information abroad. Maybe some dangers are around us we can't realize.

But if we see the TV, we can know what happened everyday around us. We can prepare to avoid the dangers.

**Sample 29:**

Nowadays, TV is very popular in our life. Almost every day we would watch TV. Generally speaking our life can't leave TV. Some one want to ask "TV is a good thing or a bad thing?" In my opinion, TV has its advantages and it also has its disadvantages.

TV is very important thing for our life. First, every day we can learn a lot of things and know many information from TV. If we didn't have TV, we could not know many world news and the china news. TV make me have many knowledge. Second, when we return home from work every night we'll be very tired. We need to relax. TV will help us to relax. I think the importance is if we have TV we would not go to other countries and we'll know other countries' customs, culture and so on. So TV is necessary to our life.

But TV also has disadvantages. Some people esp. children very like to watch TV. They spend a lot of time watching. It has effect on their study. We should spend time studying not watching. TV has a lot of advertisements. Some are good but others are bad. Not every advertisement will influence our purchase. And when some children see good toys they will ask their parents to buy. Most younger parents could not afford to buy. So TV also has its disadvantages.

Generally speaking TV is very essential to our life. We must learn to use it properly. TV will bring good for us.

**Sample 30:**

TV, which has long entered people's life, is playing a more and more important role and an indispensable part to people's daily life. It's hard to imagine that nowadays people could do away with TV at ease. But people also have long argued about it: Is TV a good thing or a bad thing?

As a product of new technology, TV apparently has many advantages. First, people could get to know daily new as quickly and lively as possible, which other means of media couldn't catch up with. Second, people could get desirable information from some ads or other programs. With the help of this information, some people, for example, could get a decent job. Third, TV is a window for world. From it we can learn up-to-date knowledge and entertain ourselves. Watching TV programs, people are always feeling relaxed.

The disadvantages of TV are also obvious. To begin with, TV programs are always full of TV-serials and tiresome advertisements, which is meaningless and a waste of money to produce and for people, a waste of time to watch. Second, there are inevitably something of violence and sex on TV, which is not suitable for children to watch. Last, safety is also a problem that really has room for improvement. The x-rays radiated by the screen are harmful to people's health, and long hours of watching is also bad for the watcher's eyes.

Despite of these disadvantages, I hold the opinion that TV is no doubt a good thing. It's a product of the progress of our society and I believe it will progress to meet needs of people.


**Sample 31:**

In my opinions, Student-center Class is a really wonderful idea.

As we all know, the classroom belongs to the teacher and the students. It is very irresponsible to leave the classroom to the teacher only. In that case, it will be difficult for students to concentrate on their studies. They will be difficult to learn new knowledge. This is very bad for their growth. It also doesn't help them develop a positive personality.

On the contrary, after we establish the student-centered classroom, our teaching level will be greatly improved. Students will be more active in asking and answering questions. The atmosphere of learning will become better and every student will experience the joy of learning. The interaction between them and teachers will become more. Teachers and students will become more open to communication.

Those are my opinions and the reason why I think so. Thank you for reading them.

**Sample 32:**

According to the understanding of the relevant content, what I know from looking it up, this educational philosophy from abroad is "student-centered". It was initially proposed by John Dewey, Switzerland educator. Switzerland, which can be said to be the core concept of western education.

I think this method is very accurate. It can stimulate students' interest in learning. Teachers can guide students to think and discuss by asking questions. This is also a reflection of the teacher's teaching level, not laissez-faire, not control. To let students choose is to make students feel that they are the masters of learning and are more willing to learn.

The significance of this teaching mode lies in 3 tips.

1 Student-centered means that students have the right to speak.

2 Student-centered means that students have the right to choose.

3 Student-centered means to fully achieve "teaching students in accordance with their aptitude".

To sum up, I think this teaching method is necessary to be applied in today's classroom.

**Sample 33:**

Universities are gradually realizing the concept of student-centered education.

I think student-centered teaching is very important, which can promote the communication between teachers and student, activate then thinking ability of students make the class more interesting, and let student learn in a happy way. Therefore, I fully support this practice. The university is student-centered. Generally speaking, it regards students as the establishment of the university. Take meeting the needs of students as the fors of the university and imporove students.

Leaning level is the primary goal of university education, taking students to participate in university affairs as the basic right of students, and establishing a close relationship with students as the major.

It is of great significance, and it is also of great significance to the development of Chinese universities.

**Sample 34:**

With the development of society, traditional teaching methods have been gradually eliminated. From teacher-centered teaching mode to student-centered.

First of all, student-centered is conducive to improving students' knowledge-seeking ability. In class, students can take the initiative to think about problems. Second, teachers can develop different characteristics and potentials of each student in teaching. Teachers should know about students' strengths and weaknesses. Guide them to achieve their goals in life. Therefore, teachers can adopt personalized teaching according to the characteristics of each student. This can promote the development of students' potential. Thirdly, taking students as the center shows the equal relationship between teachers and students. This can better promote the relationship between teachers and students. Teachers will also keep pace with the times and grow together with students.

So I agree with the student-centered teaching model. I think this new teaching method will improve the teaching level.

**Sample 35:**

I think classroom should be student-centered. because the teacher is inevitably boring, lacks life, and students-centered classroom can maximize students' ability to create capacity and think, so that students have knowledge of knowledge. More profound experience, but teachers can not indulge students, to teach entertainment and two-way proficiency, to guide students' development learning under the maximum freedom to students.

**Sample 36:**

Student-centered teaching is gradually being introduced in universities. I am about to elaborate on my views on student secondary education.

I think this kind of education is good because students are at the center of the classroom and education should revolve around students. And this can allow students to better learn and achieve the purpose of education. And I think that education can not only focus on learning. There is an old Chinese saying, first adults and then became talents. That is to say, education should pay more attention to the quality and physical and mental health of students.

And I think the significance of student-centered education is to be able to better achieve education. That is, to enable students to grow better, whether in learning or in other aspects.

**Sample 37:**

Student-centered teaching is needed in universities. Student-centered teaching is gradually being implemented in universities. I think it's good to be student-centered. Because the audience of teaching is the students. I think the significance of implementing student-centered teaching is to educate students more effectively. After entering the university, everyone made breakthroughs in their own fields. The student-centered teaching can realize this point from the center to a large extent. So here's my point. Schools need to be student-centered in teaching, and students also need schools to be student-centered in teaching. Learning is a thing that needs to be focused on. In the university, physical fitness has done a good job for us, we need to grasp the key to learn, more need to student-centered to learn. Therefore, student-centered teaching is needed in universities.

**Sample 38:**

Many universities are implementing student-centered learning. I think this kind of learning is very good. It creates a quieter learning environment for students and enables students to be more involved in learning. At the same time, taking students as the center can educate students according to their problems, so that students can accept them more easily and learn better. I advocate this kind of education. This can make students easier to accept, get rid of a variety of homework and courses, make learning more interesting, and enhance students' love of learning. In terms of teachers, it also reduces the teaching burden of teachers and avoids unnecessary trouble for schools.

I hope more school can invest in Student-centered class.

**Sample 39:**

The essence of "student-centered" is a teaching method that changes the focus of teachers' teaching into that of students' learning. In the classroom, teachers can not teach in a regular way. But students can participate in classroom learning happily. Teachers should be "Directors", while students are "actors".

The traditional teaching evaluation only pays attention to the test scores of students. I think the evaluation of "student-centered" teaching can also be diversified. Students' self-evaluation, students' mutual evaluation and teachers' evaluation. You can also pass the periodic examination, unit examination, mid-term examination and final examination. Or more simple question checking, etc. In the process of evaluation, we should pay more attention to positive praise and encourage them to put forward their own ideas, so as to make students become a new generation with thinking, ability and personality.

With the change of thought, there will be the change of practice. However, we cannot unilaterally believe that "student-centered" is perfect and "teacher-centered" is worthless. Instead, we should use diversified teaching methods according to the characteristics of the curriculum and the needs of teaching objects. So the students can study happily and master their due knowledge and learning skills.

**Sample 40:**

Through the society development, the universities are closely change their teaching ways which is the student-centered teaching.

In my opinion, it is necessary to the student-centered teaching. In 21 century, the students are needed not only the lessons, but also more reality knowledge. The knowledge in books can not satisfy with the students. The student-centered teaching can more helpful to students and makes them more outstanding after their graduated their university and walk to the normal society. What is more, they will change into the almighty people and more adapt to the rapidly developing society.

The significance of implementing student-centered teaching lies in improving students' own quality and adapt them to the normal society better. I believe that in such a teaching state, students will become more outstanding. More national talents will appear!

**Sample 41:**

Young people are the future of a country, and receiving college education helps to improve the ability of young people and many college are gradually implement student-centered teaching.

# Appendix

I'm all for student-centered teaching. Because student-oriented teaching is very helpful to students' learning, and as a student I like it very much. student-centered teaching is best for student.

Student-centered teaching helps students to learn knowledge and enhance their learning ability. It's more helpful to society. Because the school carries out student-centered education in the school days, it will help us a lot when we work. for example, it will make us more independent.

**Sample 42:**

A university is student-centered. In a word, students are the core of the university. The foundation of the university, meeting the needs of students as the focus of the university.

To improve students' learning level is the primary goal of university education. Students participate in university affairs as a basic right of students, which is built with students. This is of great significance not only to the development of Chinese university students, but also to the development of Chineseuniversities themselves.

Promotes the students as the center, strengthen the student market forces and as the power of the alumni give play to the role of the student to the university support and checks and balances. from only responsible for the government to make university is responsible for the government, is responsible for the students. to promote university ranking, the town government, government officials system of development and growth of university students.

**Sample 43:**

I am a college student. Now the university has gradually implemented the student-centered teaching method. I am very grateful.

In order to implement the concept of education and enhance China's strength. The way of education in China is constantly improving. The student-centered teaching method enables teachers to formulate more targeted learning plans for students, which will continue to improve with the students' learning situation. The school can provide different education methods for different types of students, provide different learning plans, allocate different educational resources, open more learning windows, add additional learning projects. improve students' learning ability and interest, more effectively improve students' academic performance and give full play to the school's educational ability.

The student-centered teaching method is the renewal of the old education method. Although it will spend some time to explore and some energy to improve, it can improve the school's educational ability and students will get more benefits, which is worth it.

**Sample 44:**

Students are slowly being implemented in universities, and this system is being slowly implemented. I think it has many benefits, but there are also many disadvantages. First of all, it is conducive to improving students' enthusiasm and curiosity, and at the same time can promote students to take the initiative to think and solve problems themselves. Secondly, it can also promote teamwork and enhance classmates' friendship. It can develop student subconscious, and it can create a good teacher-student relationship. One of the shortcomings is that some students are shy and unwilling to speak during group study, which will have a great impact on academic performance. At the same time, teachers may also cause a vicious circle and cause bad influence because they cannot balance all the members of the group.

However, after practice in some regions, good results have been achieved. Both students and teachers have made great progress.

**Sample 45:**

It helps cultivate students' ability to think and explore. The student centered teaching method means that the position of teachers and students changes during the teaching process. Teachers are no longer using the traditional indoctrination teaching. But more through the organization of teaching activities to cultivate students' subjects ability. This teaching method focuses on the cultivation of students' learning habits, so that students can improve their enthusiasm and initiative in learning. In the classroom, the enthusiasm of students can fully mobilize the classroom atmosphere. In a good teaching atmosphere, students can not help thinking, exploring and cultivating students' thinking and exploration ability has a certain significance.

**Sample 46:**

With the advancement of the wave of higher education reform, it has become a trend to implement the "student-centered" teaching model in universities.

In our learning process, we will use applications. They will teach according to their aptitude, and each has their own unique record of the learning process. I see student-centered teaching as an active search for adaptation to higher education.

I think this trend is positive. The 21st century is the century of knowledge economy. The popularization of the Internet makes knowledge memory no longer important. What is important is to cultivate talents who can think and innovate in the new century. Premier Li Keqiang also proposed major reform measures to promote "mass entrepreneurship and innovation" at the Davos Forum, which requires my country to reserve a large number of creative talents. This is what the traditional teaching method cannot provide, and the new learning method emphasizes the active participation of students, communication and cooperation between students, and the critical presentation of their own opinions, which is very important for new talents. Cultivation is of great benefit.

**Sample 47:**

As the college life goes on, the more we find that student-centered class teaching is gradually beings adopted in university.

In my opinion, it's a good phenomenon for students and teachers, which can made students comprehensively accept knowledge and use different teaching ways to made students think differently. At the same time, students can learn more and study independently and improve efficiency.

This way of teaching not only lightens the teacher's burden, but also enable to the students to learn more and greatly enhances their learning ability.

Therefore, I support this kind of students-centered class teaching way and hope to learn more from this kind of teaching.

**Sample 48:**

Nowadays, with the development of society, people attach more importance to the education of students. Therefore, many universities are gradually implementing student-centered class teaching methods. People also have different opinions on this teaching method.

Without a doubt, I think this teaching method is correct. Because my school places great emphasis on student-centered class, so I know this way will bring great benefits to students. First of all, Student-centered teaching can fully highlight the principal role of students in teaching activities and promote students to think about problems on their own initiative. Secondly, this way is conducive to stimulate the potential of students. it is easier to reflect the ability of students.

The significance of students-centered class lies in that it can give full play to individual value and benefit students' physical and mental health. Taking all these factors into consideration, we naturally come to the conclusion that students-centered class is feasible.

**Sample 49:**

Nowadays, universities are gradually implementing student-centered teaching, which I think is very correct, students are de main body of the school, I think. only teaching method, mode, ect. according to students ideas and opinions, can truly achieve the teaching, students give priority to, to meet them, their performance will be improved, various aspects ability will be improved, with students as the center, let them fell they are valued, let them fell the value of itself, it has a lot of benefits to their study. As long as all the policies are in line with the students themselves, the students will have more love for study and life. In the end, I think this is a very correct decision. I believe that if all the schools can achieve the real sense of student-centered. I believe there will be unexpected improvement.

**Sample 50:**

Today's universities have gradually developed a policy of student-centered teaching. With regard to the above guidelines, I extend the following personal views.

First, students are the main force in the school, and any person who is not a student in the school plays a supporting role, so it makes sense to take students as the center.

Secondly, students also want to exercise their ability in all aspects, that is, everyone is centered on you, it should be more serious and responsible, do the student's own work, diligent and upward.

In some ways, it is quite necessary to implement student-centered education, which can not only urge students to work harder, but also greatly improve their enthusiasm and make them better prepared for going out of campus.

That's my personal opinion.

**Sample 51：**

In recent years, the university is gradually implementing student-centered teaching. In my opinion, I think this is a good way. Student-centered teaching is mainly Student-centered, which will better understand student's views and ideas. Teachers will be more convenient in the process of teaching, shorten the distance between students and teachers, and enable students to improve their interest in learning. I think this is a good way for students to experience the fun of learning. As we enter the 21st century, as we grow older, our sense of autonomy is also increasing. If we study in the rigid way of teachers, we are likely to feel irritable or dislike. The student-centered teaching method will better reflect the ideas of students and make the teaching work more convenient. In my opinion, the significance of implementing student-centered reaching is to improve contemporary education methods and educational ideas. Which is also a good progress. I believe this type of education model will enable students to have a deeper understanding of what they are learning and stimulate their learning creativity. These are my views on the gradual implementation of student-centered teaching in universities.

**Sample 52：**

With the development of the economy, education is playing a more and more important role in promoting economy. Student-centered classes take place in many universities. The following are my views.

On the one hand, taking this new measures can promote efficiency of teaching by solving problems efficiently to some all, taking can provide teachers with great understanding of their students, in which they would make proper programs and assignments for students, in will have great convenience for students so that students would spend more time on their interests or professional study. On the other hand, students-centered classes may cause too much freedom for several students, which need serious consideration.

Taking all factors into consideration, advantages on student-centered are more evident. There is no doubt that student-centered classes will have a profound influence on education.

**Sample 53:**

I think student centered is a goodthing. If people want to get good grades. They should study hard, if class centered. It will make student listen class good. what about you? How do you think this view? If the class only listens teacher student will not hard for class, they will do something they want to do. So class centered for student is a good thing. Believe it or not, that can make student get good grades. I want all school like this. I think these teacher all the good teacher. I think many people want have these class.

**Sample 54:**

Student-oriented the role of teachers in students in student-centered learning problem solving Combing theory with practice. explore knowledge vocational skills and attitudes towards employment through group and independent learning activities. It support students to explore and solve problems using questioning. It support students to learn through competition and collaboration, stimulate student interaction activities to select specific outcomes assess student-centered learning. Student-centered teaching method which is a new teaching experience, is also the trend of future teaching methods. emphasizing that students are the main body in the whole teaching activity. "Student-centered teaching method" is in the open teaching environment in the autonomy of loose in a harmonious teaching environment.

Valuable questions can stimulate students' inner exploration needsM ask invite positive thinking arouse curiosity and imagination questions. Students in small group can express their opinions according to the established order of speech, full communication in-depth exploration. It helps students to clarify doubts, break through difficulties and grasp key points. And in the collision of thoughs it may produce a new discovery that the teacher did not expect. Or it may be said to be a breakthrough in thinking.

**Sample 55:**

In this day and age, there are more educational classrooms. Educational institutions are also becoming more and more sound in China. Today's educational institutions are more centered on student services. Here is my opinion on this matter.

You know, my center is important, but Students 'learning should be student-oriented, so this is very important. But teachers pay more attention to teaching students knowledge. Therefore, it is necessary to take students as the center in class, which can strengthen the state of students' concentration in class. It helps students to better put their help in the classroom and study, which can also improve students' performance.

But it can't be completely student-centered. Both are important.

**Sample 56:**

I think student-centered education has been the core educational concept since ancient times. The educational ideas of the past can still be seen in some ancient books. My opinion is as follows.

First of all, I think student-centered students can clearly understand the needs and requirements of students and the progress of the course. Second, although I think student-centered education is correct, it is important for students to learn by themselves instead of relying on teachers' ideas and concepts all the time. It's diffusion of thinking, autonomous learning, innovative learning. Finally, whether student-centered is good or bad depends on the students themselves, so it varies from person to person.

**Sample 57:**

Like the name implies, student-centered learning (SCL) makes students co-creators of their own education, engaging them in decisions about what, when, and how they learn. In doing so, SCL helps high schools prepare students not only with academic knowledge, but also with the skills of self-direction, curiosity, creativity, and collaboration they'll need for future success.

Students succeed when what they're learning matters to them. In student-centered learning, students' interest drives education. Student-centered learning gives students the opportunity to decide two things: what material they learn and how they learn it. (This concept is also sometimes referred to as personalized learning.) In contrast to teacher-centered approaches, SCL engages students as leaders and decision-makers in their own learning. For example, at Purdue Polytechnic High School in Indianapolis, students engage in SCL in their foundations class, as they solve real-world challenges posed by community partners—for example, how students would support a future world with 9.5 billion people living on it. Students plan their own research, propose a solution, communicate their ideas to teachers and community members, and evaluate their own progress as they go. Teachers help guide this process, but the content, timing, and motivation are down to students themselves.

**Sample 58:**

Nowadays, the university is gradually becoming a student-centered teaching method. In my opinion, this method can be carried out. Students are different. So everyone's way of learning is different, and there may be no way to keep up with the teacher's teaching. So the classroom should be student-centered to teach students. This may make students more receptive to knowledge. It will also make students more interested in attending classes. I think the student-centered teaching method is of great significance. He can be the students should be more receptive to knowledge, but also to make everyone Learn better. Look further. Universities are gradually implementing this approach toteaching. Students are the flowers of the motherland. Students are the most important. I think this is of great significance. So I hope that universities can achieve a student-centered teaching method.

**Sample 59:**

In the past, the bulk of classes were teacher-centered, which meant teachers talking all the time while the students were just the listeners. However, such form has changed. They let the students become more active in the classes and this is a so-called "student-centered class".

From my point of view, a student-centered class involves more students. It can catch students' attention easily. Students play an important role in the class. They can catch up with teachers' ideas more quickly. What's more, students can enhance learning and ability of creativity. This form of class needs students to be more active. Teachers are trying to motivate their enthusiasm and let students talk about their ideas freely. Creativity is very important for a university student.

Students -centered classes are more and more popularnow. This is a good trend. I believe it's a good way to teach students.

**Sample 60:**

It's so expected to think that the trend what a fresh teaching manner, the center of the university students. Agreeing with it, for that more personality to suit different children. I hope it can not only measure in the university but also in every studying environment. In the current society, personality has a strong structure. we are point it, in the studying or in a life.

As students in thestudy, it is doubly a better than before that. If we put more attention to student-self, we can see huge change what is unbelievable increase.

These are my suggestions. For one, we should be care of every students and search for their Highland. For another, we have taken a balance with teachers and students. Because every students have different level, we have to put test to know that. We must to trust it is the best way to learn knowledge.

# References

[1] BROWN, YULE. Discourse Analysis[M]. London:Cambridge University Press, 1983.

[2] CARRELL, Psychology of Language [M]. Biejing: Foreign Language Teaching and Research Press, 2000.

[3] CHARLES, LI. Thompson, Subject and Topic: A New Typology of Language[M]. London/New York: Academic Press, 1976.

[4] KRAMSCH, language and Culture, Oxford University Press, 1998.

[5] KRAMSCH. Language and Culture [M]. Beijing: Foreign Language Teaching and Research Press, 2000.

[6] COLE,SCRIBNER. Culture and Thought: A Psychological Introduction [M]. New York: John Wiley, Inc, 1974.

[7] Corder, S. Pit. Introducing Applied Linguistics [M].Middlesex: Penguin, 1973.

[8] BATES,PLOG. Cultural Anthropology[M]. McGraw Hill, 1990.

[9] CARROLL. Psychology of language [M]. Foreign Language Teaching and Research Press, 2000.

[10] BOLINGER, SEARS. Aspects of Language [M]. Harcourt Brace Jovanovich, Inc, 1981.

[11] NIDA. Language, Culture and Translating [M].Inner Mongolia University Press, 1998.

[12] NIDA. Language, Culture and Translating [M]. Shanghai:Shanghai Foreign Language Education Press, 1993.

[13] FUNG. A Short History of Chinese Philosophy [M]. Free Press, 1997.

[14] YULE. The Study of Language [M]. Foreign Language Teaching and Research

# References

Press, 2000.

[15]GUMPERZ. LEVINSON. Rethinking linguistic relativity [M]. Cambridge: Cambridge University Press. 1996.

[16]ISHII, SATOSI. Thought patterns as modes of rhetoric: the United States and Japan [M]. California: Wadsworth Publishing Company, 1985.

[17] HARMER. How to Teach English [M]. Foreign Language Teaching and Research Press, 2000.

[18]VENUTI. The Translation Studies Reader [M]. London, New York, 2000.

[19] LEECH, SVARTVIK. A Communicative Grammar of English (2nd ed.) [M]. Longman, 1994.

[20]BEAMER,VARNER. Intercultural Communication in the Global Workplace, McGraw-Hill/Irwin, 2000.

[21]DAVIS. Doing Culture Cross-cultural Communication in Action [M]. Foreign Language Teaching and Research Press, 2001.

[22] MATALENE. Contrastive Rhetoric: An American Writing Teacher in China [M]. College English, 1985.

[23] MCCREA, KEMMERLE. College Writing [M]. The Bobbs-Merrill Company, Inc., 1985.

[24]NAKAMURA. Ways of Thinking of Eastern Peoples [M]. Honolulu, 1964.

[25] Pribram, Karl. Conflicting Patterns of Thought [M]. Washington: Public Affairs Press, 1949.

[26]QUIRK.et al., A Grammar of Contemporary English [M].London: Longman, 1973.

[27] ROBINS. General Linguistics. Fourth edition [M]. Foreign Language Teaching and Research Press, 2000.

[28]RALPH. The Sociolingustics of Language [M]. Beijing: Foreign Language Teaching and Research Press, 2000.

[29] ROBERT. Language Learning "Cultural thought patterns in intercultural education" [M].Blackwell Publishers, 1966.

[30]ROBERT. A comparative study of Chinese and western cyclic myths [M].New York: Peter Lang Publishing Inc., 1992.

[31] SAMOVAR. Communication between Cultures [M]. Belmont: Wadsworth Pub.

Co.，1991.

[32]SAPIR. Language，Harcourt[M].Brace & World，Inc，1970.

[33]STEWART. American Cultural Patterns：A Cross-cultural Perspective[M].Chicago：Intercultural Press Inc.，1981.

[34]STUART C. Poole. An Introduction to Linguistics[M].Foreign Language Teaching and Research Press，2000.

[35]ULLA. Contrastive Rhetoric Cross-cultural Aspects of Second Language Writing[M]. Shanghai Foreign Language Educational Publishing House，2001.

[36]WHORF. Language，Thought and Reality[M]. Massachusetts Institute of Technology，1956.

[37]YOUNG. Intercultural Personhood：An Integration of Eastern and Western Perspectives[M].L. Samovar & R. Porter (Eds.)，1994.

[38]ZENO. "Wordless Thoughts" in William C. & McCormack et al：Language and Thought：Anthropological Issues[M]. Paris：Mouton Publishers，1977.

[39]WANG. Chinese Grammar Theory[M].Jinan:Shandong Education Press，1984.

[40]蔡基刚.英汉写作对比研究[M].上海:复旦大学出版社,2001.

[41]陈安定.英汉比较与翻译[M].北京:中国对外翻译出版公司,1998.

[42]狄艳华.美国文化[M].长春:吉林科学技术出版社,2002.

[43]冯兰.跨文化背景下中西方英语学术论文写作差异研究[J].重庆第二师范学院学报.2015(05).

[44]桂诗春.心理语言学[M].上海:上海外语教育出版社,1985.

[45]何善芬.英汉语言对比研究[M].上海:上海外语教育出版社,2002.

[46]胡壮麟.语言学教程[M].北京:北京大学出版社 ,2017

[47]胡壮麟,刘润清,李延福.语言学教程[M].北京:北京大学出版社,1987.

[48]贾德江.英汉语对比研究与翻译[M].北京:国防科技大学出版社,2002.

[49]连淑能.英汉对比研究[M].北京:高等教育出版社,1993.

[50 李宏强.大学生英语写作与母语思维的相关性研究[J].高教学刊.2019(17).

[51]刘宓庆.汉英对比研究的理论问题(下)[J].外国语,1991(5):46-50.

[52]孟建钢.英语普通语言学教程[M].长沙:湖南人民出版社,2003.

[53]潘文国.汉英语对比纲要[M].北京:北京语言文化大学出版社,1997.

[54]彭宣维.英汉语篇综合对比[M].上海:上海外语教育出版社,2000.

[55]邵志洪.英汉语研究与对比[M].上海:华东理工大学出版社,1997.

[56]申小龙.中国句型文化[M].长沙湖南教育出版社,1997.

[57]唐德根.跨文化交际学[M].中南工业大学出版社 2000.

[58]王寅.英汉语言宏观结构区别特征,外国语,1990(6).

[59]王钢. 普通语言学基础[M].长沙:湖南教育出版社,1987.

[60]王瑛.中西方思维模式差异与大学英语教学[J].科技视界.2015(34).

[61]王昱钦.中西方思维模式差异与大学英语教学[J].海外英语.2016(20).

[62]张爱琳.跨文化交际[M].重庆:重庆大学出版社,2003.

[63]张光明.英汉互译思维概论[M].北京:外语教学与研究出版社,2001.

[64]张光明.名作赏析导论[M].北京:军事谊文出版社,1999.

[65]张忠利,宗文举.中西文化概论[M].天津:天津大学出版社,2002.

[66]郑春苗.中西文化比较研究[M].北京:北京语言学院出版社,1994.

[67]朱俊.略论母语思维对英语学习者的影响[J].中小学英语教学与研究.2008 (6):15-17.